_10/n /23_

To: Lisa,
May this Book ccrry ts
Much pleasure as Meeting you has
Brought Me!
Skeeter
Mance

Bedtime Stories for GROWN-UPS

www.skeetermance.com

LARRY "SKEETER" MANCE

MW00612345

ISBN: 978-1-955622-77-6

Copyright © 2021 by Larry "Skeeter" Mance

All rights reserved. No part of this publication may be reproduced, distributed, or transmitted in any form or by any means, including photocopying, recording, or other electronic or mechanical methods without the prior written permission of the publisher. For permission requests, solicit the publisher via the address below.

Skeeter Mance.com LLC
Taccoa, GA 30577

Printed in the United States of America

Table of Contents

Foreword

Dr. Charles Liotta
GA Tech Vice Provost, Professor of Chemistry

In this series of autobiographical short stories, Skeeter has presented himself as a strong witness for the presence of Christ in his life. The short stories are, in fact, an evangelical experience. The reader is brought face-to-face with the fact that Christ is an integral part of our lives during the good times and the bad. He reveals himself in the words and actions of the most unlikely individuals. While the stories deal with events that Skeeter has experienced, there is a universal message for each and every reader. If we acknowledge that Christ is our lord and savior, we will readily recognize that the good and bad events we experience are *teachable moments* that Christ provides to allow us to grow spiritually. *Skeeter is correct!* The universal character *"Itsunme"* is in fact "You and Me."

—Dr. Charles Liotta

About the Author

Cornell T. Seymour
Chemical Engineer, Saudi Aramco (Retired)

I first met Skeeter in 1970 (he later became Rev. Larry D. Mance in 1986), when we were freshmen at the Georgia Institute of Technology in Atlanta, Georgia. He was an aerospace-engineer major but went two years later to the School of Industrial Management after funding and jobs were cut in the US space industry. We were a small group of fifty black students in a sea of more than ten thousand white students and were quite invisible in the fabric of the daily life at Tech (the Harvard of the South). He was living in the Smith dormitory with Atty. Jerry Washington (his roommate), "Sam" Johnson, Jerry "Bird" Wilson (who later became his roommate), Harry Crew, Dr. Zedrick "Zed" Holloway, James "Jimmy" McCormick, James "Geech" Grant, and several other black students. It was Sam Johnson who gave him the nickname Skeeter, and he gave it to him because he was only about 110 to 120 pounds and quite energetic (some might even say "hyper") and seemed to buzz around like a mosquito. Sam felt that one of his duties in life was to give all of us nicknames. The name seemed fitting, and everyone we knew started calling him Skeeter; in the end, he accepted it and embraced it as a stage name. He possessed a unique quality that was clearly noticeable. Many of us thought that he just merely had the gift of gab, but as time went on, we discovered that he had so much more. On October 1971, with the help of Jane Willey (the student-center director) and Don Nelson (a professor and board member of *Humanics Press*), he distinguished himself by performing Tech's first poetry recital that was set to music at the GA Tech Student Center before an audience of over two hundred people from GA Tech, Spelman College, Morehouse College, Morris Brown College, and Clark University. This performance appeared as an article in the *Technique* (GA Tech's student-body newspaper) and later got his poems published in the *Erato* (Tech's literary-magazine publication). He was never selfish and has always shared his venues with other aspiring artists who lacked exposure. Skeeter asked Benjamin "The Raven" Davis (a friend and one of the fifty) to perform during his intermission; it used Skeeter's three-piece contemporary-jazz combo, which consisted of Eric Johnson (bass), Donald "Jump" Jumper (piano/keyboards), and Richard "King-Tutt" Ware (drums and percussions).

Somehow we all lost touch with one another. I went on to pursue a career as a chemical engineer with Aramco, and he ended up getting married to the love of his life, Gwendolyn McChriston of Spelman College (she's from Mobile, Alabama). In the following year, he enlisted in the US Air Force. During the Vietnam War, he was stationed at Clark AFB in the Philippine Islands, serving as an avionics specialist that maintained the flight instruments in the cockpits of the F-4 fighter bombers and the C-130 cargo planes. They had three children (TaMeesha, Aurious, and Alesha).

That experience was life-changing for him. In God's own way, He was making Skeeter realize the great gift that He had bestowed upon him. Through our struggles, we often wonder "Why is God doing this to me?" But Larry persevered. He returned to the Tech in 1974 and continued his study in the School of Industrial Management. He left again in 1976 after doing his second poetry recital at the GA Tech Student Center. Finally, after several years, he reentered Tech after all his children were adults/emancipated. He graduated in 1997, and at age 46, he became Tech's oldest undergraduate student to obtain a BS degree and the second person in the school's history to obtain a bachelor's degree past the age of forty.

It was an awesome moment of pride and distinction, yes, but the pains of war had left emotional scars and bitter memories that would plague him to this day. It was during these trying times that he returned to the simple truth that his loving parents had taught him when he was a young boy growing up in Toccoa, Georgia. That simple truth is the sincere love for and worship of our Heavenly Father.

Skeeter became a minister after receiving his calling in 1986. His beautiful messages were strictly Bible-based with a generous mixture of life experiences. Those who were fortunate enough to hear his masterfully delivered sermons were amazed by the fact that one so young could be so knowledgeable of God's Word. On one occasion, while on vacation from Saudi Arabia, I even had a chance to surprise him as he delivered the Word to a Methodist congregation in Acworth, Georgia.

Several months ago, he began a serious work that had been burdening him for years. He wrote a book that was dedicated to teaching listeners about the sincere value of their worth to God and of their heartfelt praise. These stories provide opportunities for us to better understand God's purpose in and for our lives. They provide an effective, edifying platform to instruct others (especially children from ages 7 to 17) about biblical, godly values and principles.

Purchasing this book is a very wise choice, indeed, and a decision you will never regret. You will find that the stories embedded in these pages are not only intriguing but also thought-provoking, humorous, and sentimental. As you read the stories, you will begin to know and experience this great and anointed author of our generation.

—Cornell T. Seymour

Preface

From the outset, I want to thank Yahweh (Almighty God the Father) and His beloved Son, **Yeshua Hamashiach** (Jesus Who Is the Christ), because I could not have written and produced *Teachable Moments* without their grace and mercy. I almost died twice within five years and am supposed to be dead, but I cried out in prayer, and they heard me and granted me the time I needed to see this project come to fruition. The miraculous incidents mentioned will be detailed in my autobiography, *So Much Left Unsaid,* which is to be published later. I am a service-connected, disabled Vietnam War veteran and a true believer who has seen and experienced the reality of God since I was four years old. He has given me an abundance of gifts and talents, and I seek to utilize them to their fullest potentials, for the Word says, "For unto whomsoever much is given, of him shall be much required: and to whom men have committed much, of him they will ask the more" (Luke 12:48). I believe the greatest tragedy of life is for a flower to bud but never blossom; we have too many people (especially young people) who do that. Hopefully, this book will inspire many to find the hope and motivation necessary to accomplish their dreams (no matter how late in the day it may seem). My books (*Teachable Moments* and *Bedtime Stories for Grown-Ups*) are designed for husbands to read to wives and vice versa at bedtime and also for children to read to parents (or loved ones) who are in hospitals, hospices, nursing homes, and/or assisted-living centers. It's a great means for children who wish to read to parents, grandparents, and/or siblings and increase their knowledge of God as well as their reading skills.

This book is dedicated to my father, B. C. Mance (May 30, 1914); my mother, Millie Mance (Dec. 24, 1919–Nov.11, 2013); my sister and surrogate mother, Pearlena Mance-Askew; and my good friends and fellow veterans Joseph Davis (Apr. 20, 1948–Feb. 19, 2014) and Charles Warren Smith, as well as Vera Campbell and Marti Martin.

Special thanks are extended to Ms. F. K. Walther (my primary editor), whom God sent to help me birth both books (*Teachable Moments* and *Bedtime Stories for Grown-Ups*). I also want to thank Dr. Charles Liotta, Dr. Philip Adler, Cornell Seymour, and Bonnie Mance-Brown.

The purpose of this book is to edify (lift up), educate, and motivate its reader. It intends to increase the reader's awareness of the reality of God, to strengthen their faith, and to motivate them to have a greater, more intimate relationship with God and Christ.

I recommend that you read this book one story at a time, pausing after each and contemplating what has been written and what's really being said at the end. This book is written to make you think by giving you modern-day parables that emphasize biblical teachings and principles. Research has gone into the writings, and if you will read the book in the recommended way, pieces of the puzzle of the Bible will begin to fall into place, thus increasing your understanding of the Word of God.

It occurred to me that there wasn't a Christian storybook for adults. Therefore, I thought it was fitting and proper to write a book that husbands and wives could read to each other at bedtime; it's also a book that children can read to their parents or relatives in nursing homes, hospitals, assisted-living centers, and hospices. The appropriateness of each story in the book is left up to its reader as some of the stories are beyond the interest and understanding of children. I hope the materials in the book will be used for Sunday school classes, Vacation Bible School, and Christian study groups. You will also find poems that are excerpts that were taken from *Something from the Heart but for the Soul* (a collection of my poetry that is to be published at a later date).

Oftentimes, one will begin to read a book, but an interruption occurs, breaking the reader's concentration. Both books have been deliberately structured with that in mind and are ideal for reading while waiting in bathrooms, barbershops, beauty salons, hospitals, waiting rooms, planes, trains, or buses; a story can be completed in a relatively short period of time. Lastly, I want to thank you, the reader, for choosing to read and investigate *Bedtime Stories for Grown-Ups*. It is my prayer that you will not be disappointed and will share this book and its concepts with your friends, families, associates, and even your enemies!

—Larry "Skeeter" Mance

The Coin

By Larry "Skeeter" Mance

Many years ago, a 7 year old girl named Colleen was visiting her grandmother for a weekend. She always loved to go to the country for she had more freedom and safety being a child. She didn't have to worry about being abducted or being shot by some kid or adult who had "lost their marbles" for God knows why. She didn't have to be concerned about traffic and could ride her bike either to the playground or the corner store; neither did she have to wait for the ice-cream truck to show up for her 'Nana' always kept and assortment of flavors of ice-cream, Popsicles, pushups, and the like either in the refrigerator or the deep freezer. Nana was a retired postal worker and Sunday school teacher but that's neither here nor there. One day while at the playground, Colleen found a half dollar coin (a Kennedy if my memory is correct) and she was dying to spend it. She stopped by the corner neighborhood candy lady's house for some gummy bears and a "*now and laters*" or two; but when she handed the lady her found money the candy lady told her that it wasn't any good. "Why not?" asked Colleen and the lady told her to ask her grandmother. Well, that just beat all and Colleen was not to be out done or cheated out of her chance to spend that money. Since she found it, it was just as good as if she had worked a 40-hour week and earned it. Nonetheless, she raced home like she was racing the speed of light with pigtails flying horizontally in the wind. I would not be a bit surprised if she a bug or two splattered on her forehead like those on the windshield of a car. It was a good thing that the local police didn't see her for she may have complicated the situation even further by getting a speeding ticket.

Nana could see that the child was upset and out of breath not just from her demeanor but also her tone.

"Nana", she megaphoned, "you won't believe what just happened". Colleen went on to explain everything from finding the coin, to trying to purchase candy and later breaking the sound barrier to get home.

"Well let me see the coin," insisted Nana "Oh, that's the problem".

"What is it Nana?" questioned Colleen.

"It's a two head coin and not legal tender," explained Nana.

"Of course its not chicken Nana. I was at the candy lady's house not McDonalds ordering from the dollar menu" volcano-ed Colleen.

Nana just laughed realizing that the only "tender" Colleen had been exposed to was chicken tenders. Nana showed her that the coin had two heads and not a tail. She informed Colleen that, in order for her money to be legitimate and not counterfeit, the coin had to have a head and a tail, a front and a back and not two fronts or two backs. Anyway, she sat Colleen down and began to tell her a story about an agnostic coin collector who had traveled the world seeking to acquire the most valuable coin on the planet. He was a person who did not deny the existence of God but neither did he have the desire or inclination to discover Him and to get to know Him personally. It's like knowing a lot about President O'Bama or Bush but never having met them in person. The man had traveled Europe, China, North & South America, Africa, Australia and so forth. During his travels he met another collector; and after bragging about his kugerands and other valuable pieces, the man told him that there was a blind man living in Tibet (named Reveileb) who possessed the most valuable coin in the world. Well, that meant that he had to change his itinerary and go there to find this man for his life long dream from childhood was to possess the most valuable coin on earth. After a few weeks of trek and inquiry he finally arrived at Reveileb's home on a Yak. After exchanging greetings and pleasantries, he was invited into Reveileb's hut where they had tea along with his expensive interpreter.

"I hear you have the most valuable coin on the planet and I'm here to buy it so name your price" said the collector.

"I cannot sell it," responded Reveileb

"$1 M dollars" said the collector. But Reveileb shook his head.

"$10 M", another headshake was the response.

$1B" and that's my final offer stated the collector.

Then Reveileb stood up walking out of the hut beaconing them to follow. And with the sun shining on the snowcaps of the Himalayas he seated himself along with the visitors. He then said "Look out there and tell me what you see; do you not see the beauty of the mountain, or smell the freshness of the air? The coin I possess I cannot sell for it is a gift that does not belong to me given to all mankind who will receive it rather than turn it down. And who ever heard of buying a gift that someone gives you? What you behold is a gift that is priceless and is not for sale. So is the coin I have and the one you seek for it is the 'Coin of Salvation'. The Bible says 'For God so loved the world that He Gave His Only Begotten Son that whosoever believeth on Him should not perish but have everlasting life'. He also said 'to them that Believe, gave He also the power to become sons of God'. You see the some total of your collection cannot buy you eternity nor pay your way into heaven.

"But how is Salvation like a coin" asked the collector

Reveileb instructed "Salvation has a two fold purpose just a coin has two sides. The first purpose is to be made into the likeness of Christ (the head of the coin) and the second is to receive eternal life (the tail of the coin). So many Christians are so concerned about living forever that they have no interest or regard to being conformed into the image of Christ; and as a result, their lives remain unchanged and they become religious robots who go to church riddled with hatred, anger, un-forgiveness, greed, jealousy, and so forth. It is impossible to meet Christ and remain the same for something must and will change. If you don't believe me then ask the Apostle Paul".

With tears in her eyes Nana said "This touched the collector in a very special way and caused him to want the coin of salvation rather than merely possess it. For the first time in his life he began to see the cause of his emptiness, his despair and lack of fulfillment. He now desired to know God and not just know about him. He returned home and gave away most of his fortune; later on the Lord called him into the ministry and his obsession changed from collecting coins to ferrying souls to the foot of the cross. His desire (until the day he died) was to eradicate counterfeit religion from the church and inform people that Salvation has a two fold purpose like a coin of legal, legitimate tender; And last but not least', she said, 'That man was your Grandfather".

You see, Salvation is a gift not based on the things we do (right or wrong) or the things we omit to do; but rather it is based on what Christ did for us all…. He died and rose so we might have life and have it more abundantly. Therefore, none of can boast about what we did or didn't do in order to enter into the Kingdom of God. Everybody is saved because of what Christ did but not all of us have accepted the gift of Salvation and, therefore, will not enter into the Kingdom.

Most of us either do not know or ignore the two-fold purpose of Salvation. There is a difference between being a creature of God and a child of God (i.e., son or daughter). Many of us want eternal life and remain the same rather than be changed into the likeness of Christ. We can never be Christ but we can seek to be changed into the likeness of His image by turning the other cheek, loving our fellowmen like Christ loved us, and, finally, by making the Father first and foremost in our lives. The only way to be conformed into the likeness of His image is to allow the Holy Spirit to take control of our hearts, our minds and our lives for we cannot be the "potter and be on the potter's wheel" at the same time. Actors and Actresses are made up all the time to look like the part they play; but their appearance and demeanor lasts only until the play or movie is over and thus temporary. But when we are born again and changed into the image of Christ (a little bit at a time) the result is permanent and reflects so in our character, outlook, behavior and attitudes. Counterfeit religion is when we love the act of serving God more than we love God Himself. This is what the Church of Laodecia in the book of Revelations was guilty of. The body of believers (i.e., the Church) was more concerned about serving on committees, volunteering at soup kitchens, helping out at the nursing homes that they were about spending time alone with God seeking His face. They had become casualties of ***"the busy demon"*** being too busy in the ***act*** of serving God that they no longer had time to spread the Love of God or to seek His face. How many Christians do you know religiously perform duties in the Church and still have issues with their fellowmen because of the color of their skin or socio-economic status? How many sing on the choir or usher and still hate their brother, mother, father, sister and look down on the homeless, the unemployed, the uneducated and "the lost"? These are signs of the counterfeit ***coins*** of Salvation.

The End

It may have been different if he had known then what he knew now, but alas, it was too late, for Rudy, who was a bully while he lived, had crossed over into the spirit world, where all the things in the Bible are real and true. Now every pleasure he got from bullying became a volcano of regret and remorse. Being stationed in the waiting room of the Judgment, he had the time to reflect on his actions on earth and to analyze what went wrong. Standing by his side was one of his guardian angels, who was assigned by Metatron (Heaven's secretary) to record his thoughts, decisions, and actions. More importantly, the angel was present to help him see things he never would have while he was alive. Out of all the people he had bullied (including his own mother) was a kid called Darnell (who was the epitome of nerdiness). Rudy came from a single-welfare-parent home, never knew his father, and was always envious of other kids who had the love and support of their families. He lived in the projects around the corner from Darnell, who had observed him strike his mother many times from the age of seven years old. His mother always upheld him in his wrongs and was quick to assault other adults in the community who tried to counsel or correct Rudy's disrespectful and unacceptable behaviors (everything from cussing to fighting). In his adult life, Rudy's nephew shot him in his foot because he violently attacked and beat up his grandmother (Rudy's mother). Rudy walked with a limp because of the injury until the day he died.

Darnell continued to suffer in his adult life from Rudy's bullying, having nightmares of being beaten up by him from time to time. When he was in his forties or fifties, Darnell prayed to God to remove the emotional and psychological scars caused by Rudy and the nightmares that persisted even after Rudy's death, and God granted his request. He even asked that Rudy not only be forgiven but that God would find room for him (Rudy) in His service on the other side. I think it must have been then that the guardian angel sent by Metatron appeared to him to help him understand and see the damage he caused so his soul wouldn't be lost. Rudy was given the chance by Almighty God in Heaven to truly repent by making amends as best as he could from Heaven's waiting room. Darnell had a son called Gizzmoe, who was having trouble with his own bully, and Rudy was given the opportunity to help Gizzmoe. But the angel first had to enlighten Rudy about what bullying is, what it causes, and just how detrimental it is to the bully despite the hurt, pain, and anguish it causes a victim. The angel asked Rudy if he knew what a bully is, and Rudy said no. The angel then said, "Rudy, a bully is an overbearing person who habitually badgers, assaults, and intimidates another person physically, emotionally, and/or psychologically with the objective to dominate and control them through fear. The person he or she intimidates is either weaker, smaller, or both. The bully has an innate jealousy or envy caused by some awful pain that he or she is too afraid to face or deal with. They usually have no one they can turn to in order to help them deal with the inner crisis they are experiencing. They feel insecure, inadequate, unwanted, unaccepted, or unloved and seek to inflict pain on others in order to feel better themselves, but that never works, for the hole inside them grows larger, and nothing seems to be able to fill it. The methods they use to deal with the emptiness inside them only exacerbate the emotional distress and crisis that bubble up inside their heart. Bullying comes from a controlling spirit. The spirit exercises great influence over the bully and seeks to have power and control over others through him. It is a demonic spirit that wants to dominate and destroy others by influencing the bully to do so.

"Because there's no relief, the bully becomes angry, hostile, violent, and unremorseful, justifying his or her actions based on what has been done or is being done to him or her. They deem it fair because they think they shouldn't experience and feel what they're feeling alone. Therefore, they believe it is all right to make someone else feel what they're feeling. Too often bullies create other bullies, just as child molesters create future molesters. Many times the bully will go home and bully younger or weaker siblings. Their method of intimidation can easily carry on into adulthood, and they end up bullying their spouses, their children, or even their elderly parents."

Gizzmoe was thirteen years old and geekier than his dad was at that age. He lived in Connecticut, not too far from Sandy Hook, and was plagued with bully problems that were beginning to become insurmountable. He had a social-studies assignment; he had to write a social-studies paper and present it before the class during his fifth period. He did not know what to write about, and his thoughts were fragmented and jagged because he was busy with thinking about how he would deal with his bully on the way home. That Monday, on his way home from school, he managed to make it past the place where his bully patrolled; the bully stayed home because of the flu and was simply waiting for him. A bad snowstorm hit the town that night; it was so bad that the school would only start again three days later because the town had to deal with the downed trees and power lines that were everywhere. Phasel and MeeMee, Gizzmoe's younger brother and sister, were bouncing off the walls the next day, running through the house and being overjoyed because there was no school. Gizzmoe treated them viciously and sometimes violently and with intolerance. Gizzmoe had both the paper and the bully on his mind constantly. They were beginning to become afraid of him, and his parents noticed that. His dad cautioned him about his attitude and behavior, mentioning that he, Gizzmoe, was not being himself, but his dad had no idea that the pain of being bullied was beginning to take its toll on his son.

The next day was full of sunshine. Almost a hundred thousand residents were without power, and schoolkids everywhere were delighted and having fun. Gizz and his brother and his sister were no exceptions. After a morning of snowball fights and making snowmen and snow angels, they thought they would do something different to chase away the monotony. They found a heavily corrugated cardboard box that once held a refrigerator and decided to turn it into a snow sled-bus. After using an old ladder, the front and back wheels and axels of his baby brother's wagon, some rope, and a few two-by-fours and four-by-sixes on the contraption, the bus became operational and ready for its maiden voyage. The game was on, and they had a great time for quite a while. Gizzmoe had the bright idea of taking it to Monster Hill for a cruise. Monster Hill was this enormous slope at the edge of the backyard that descended thirty yards at a twenty-five-degree angle down to the river (which was now frozen over) that ran through the back of the property. His brother and sister were too scared to be a part of the trial run; they refused even though Gizzmoe taunted and intimidated them. Being the thrill seeker that he was, Gizz refused to back down, and it was on like Donkey Kong.

He climbed into the contraption and gave his siblings the signal to push. Everything was going according to plan for the first eight to ten feet or so, but suddenly, the bus seemingly hit an uncalculated gear and accelerated beyond his expectation, jetting his dreadlocks straight into a 180-degree angle. The rush was like nothing he could ever imagine, and the speed, the cold, and the adrenaline were all in his face. It was like he was Jet Skiing in an open spaceship. As he zoomed down the embankment, he suddenly had a thought: *What if the ice on the river won't support my weight?* He decided to veer off to the right to avoid drowning or freezing to death. About fifteen feet from the end of the course, he snatched the rope and pulled it toward the right in an effort to drive his homemade sled away from disaster. The sled tried to obey his wish and was making the turn, but the speed caused him to roll over and smash into a huge pine tree headfirst without a helmet. Phasel, who was standing at the top of the hill, could see that what happened wasn't good and told MeeMee to get their mom while he ran as best as he could to aid Gizzmoe. Gizz, now unconscious, lay on the ground, his head bleeding. Phasel, crying and panic-stricken, called out his name. His mom and MeeMee came running toward him after calling their dad and 911.

Darnell's job was only five minutes away from the hospital, and he was waiting when the ambulance arrived. Like clockwork, the paramedics unloaded Gizz from the ambulance and rushed him into the emergency room. It was touch and go for a while, but finally, the physician on duty came out and informed the parents that Gizz had a severe concussion and was in a coma—one that he might not come out of. The whole family began to pray. Now it was to Almighty God. While in the comatose state, Gizzmoe was in a realm that words cannot describe. He heard a voice calling him from inside a bright light, and as he approached the light, a figure stepped outside its brilliance and engaged him in conversation.

Gizzmoe was afraid, and it showed as he asked the entity, "Who are you, and where am I?"

The entity replied, "I am Zamiel, and my name means 'Told by God.' You are in a realm between life and death—between your world and the next—and it is located between the light and the dark. I have come to help you while there is still time, for you are at a pivotal point in your life. You are struggling with things you have yet to understand. But before I begin, I want to introduce you to someone."

Rudy stepped forward.

"This is Rudy, and he wants to talk to you about something dear to him."

"Hi, Rudy," said Gizzmoe.

Darnell was sitting next to Gizzmoe's hospital bed when he heard him call out Rudy's name. Just the sound of the name caused the dad to remember the trauma of his childhood, and each memory was like a spider web that he got stuck in. Was it not enough that he had to endure Rudy in life? Did he have to be haunted by him now too? Was his nemesis now reaching out from beyond the grave to emotionally torture and taunt him through the event of his son's demise? These were questions that he had no answer to.

"Gizzmoe," said Rudy, "I understand you have a bully problem, and I'm here to help you understand some things about it. In life, I was the epitome of a bully. I bullied everyone I could while I was alive, but it's only now that I realize just how much I was hurting and didn't know why. I'm still not really sure why, but I think it was because I did not have a father, like so many boys around me did, and the ones who did not have a dad like me at least knew who their father was, and I'm ashamed to say that I did not. I had no sense of belonging, and I was the youngest of three children in a family that existed on welfare. My mother was a hell-raiser and fought with many men and women in the neighborhood and town over nothing. I will say that she was quick to defend me when I was doing wrong and would not allow neighbors, teachers, or anyone else to discipline me. She wouldn't even discipline me herself. I fought her from the time I was four years old. When I was a teenager, I used to bully her, and I would beat her up if she did not give me money or if someone else made me angry during my day. I guess there's a lot to be said about 'Spare the rod, spoil the child' [Proverbs 13:24]. I used to be jealous and envious of other kids who had more toys, had better clothes, and most of all, seemed to be loved by their parents. 'Why can't I have that?' I used to wonder, and it made me hateful and violent. I thought that inflicting pain on others was the right way to cope with my insecurities and shortcomings, but I was wrong. Are you being mean to your younger brother and sister?"

Gizzmoe dropped his head in shame, for Rudy had struck a nerve. "Yes, I suppose so."

Rudy went on. "That's the thing about bullying that I hate the most now, and it is the greatest harm that it does to its victims. It is not uncommon for the victims of bullying to become bullies themselves, just as children who are molested oftentimes become future molesters themselves. So the cycle of bullying repeats itself. Sometimes, there's someone in a victim's circle of influence—a sibling, a parent, a cousin, a family member, a scout leader, or a friend—who can help the victim find the courage or resources necessary to stand up to the bully and gain the insight needed to deal with a painful situation. But often a victim feels isolated. There are victims who feel so trapped that the only optimal solution they see, unfortunately, is suicide. I lived my life that way, and I am saddled with remorse, regret, and shame for the things I've done. I thought bullying gave me power and control over my victims. Instead, it only increased my hurt and pain—not only in life but also in death. I can't change what I've done, but you still have the time and the opportunity to do so. Don't follow my path or the path of the victims who did not seek help in dealing with people like me. Go to someone and talk with him or her about what you're going through, and I'm willing to bet you that everything will work out fine. Are you a believer in God and Christ? If you are, then you must believe God and trust that He will not deny you any good thing [Psalm 34:10; Joshua 21:45]. Whatever promises He makes, He will certainly honor, for He is not a man that He should lie [Numbers 23:19]. Even if you're only observing someone else being bullied, get involved by going to your parents, your principal, your teacher, or your school counselor and letting them know, for you are your brother's keeper, and you have a responsibility as a believer and child of the living God to stand against evil and the things that are wrong in your life, your home, your school, and your community."

Zamiel interrupted the conversation. He told Gizz that it was time for him to go back and reminded him that he had a responsibility to see and act on the greater good in bullying situations for the sake of the victim, the bully, and the potential future victims. Gizzmoe then whizzed back to the third dimension, and he found himself in a hospital bed with a black eye and a monster headache.

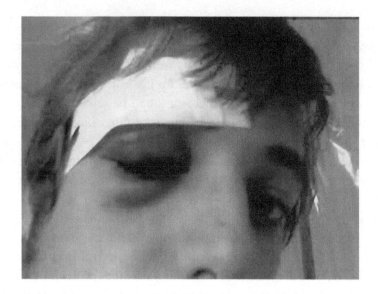

His mom, who was seated by his bedside, jumped and praised God when she saw him open his good eye; the other one was completely shut. After calming down, she drew her cell phone to tell his dad and his siblings the good news. It had been forty-eight hours since his accident, and his parents were taking shifts so he would not be alone. Well, I guess what my dad always said to me is true: "Love is not what love says. Love is what love does." Anyway, he was going to be all right in more ways than one could imagine, for the experience he had between the worlds would become a truly life-changing experience. Before, he had no idea what his social-studies paper would be about, but now, he knew. He was determined to start writing as soon as his headache would go away. Within thirty minutes, Darnell, Phasel, and MeeMee arrived, and not even Kodak could capture the love that filled the room as the family crisis subsided. Yes, their prayers had been answered in more ways than one. Gizzmoe asked his mom and dad to step outside the room and give him some time alone with his brother and sister, and of course, they obliged. He apologized to Phasel and MeeMee and told them how much he loved them. He then told them of his experience between the worlds and talked to them about bullying and all the things he learned about it. He explained to them that he could not always protect them but he could always empower them to handle life situations as best as he could. Within twenty-four hours, Gizz was discharged. Although his sled was in shambles, his mind wasn't, and he spent the rest of the week resting, collecting his thoughts, and writing his paper, which was due on the weekend.

The weekend flew by as fast as a peregrine falcon dropping down on a baby roadrunner on the Mojave Desert from five thousand feet. Gizzmoe—black eye and all—was ready to present his paper.

On Monday, Gizzmoe stood before his class ready to present his paper.

"Let me begin by saying that bullying is not always physical. It can be emotional, psychological, or even spiritual. Regardless of its type, it's always tormenting and painful. Every David has at least one Goliath in his life, and many of us have even more. Sometimes I think it's almost a rite of passage, especially for Christians. I think that God the Father creates circumstances for us to deal with in order to not only teach us and help us grow but also to make us realize and understand that He is with us and will perform His Word in our lives, just like He said He would do. We have to learn to have courage and find comfort and solace in Christ by being doers of the Word, for 'I can do all things through Christ which strengtheneth me' [Philippians 4:13]. That means we have to try it God's way, not our own way. It might not make sense, and it might appear to even be useless or futile, but we have to strive to live the Word of God and not just profess to do so on Sundays or at Christmas and Easter. There will come a time when we must take a stand [Joshua 24:15]. There have been far too many suffering people and far too many suicides because we were either too afraid or too apathetic to confront a situation or a bully. We victims must bear some responsibility for what happens not only to us but also to our siblings, our friends, and even strangers. People will continue to be bullied to *death* if we don't make an effort to take a stand against it. You don't have to be the one being bullied to report and stand against it. If you see someone who's drunk get behind the wheel of a car, what would you do? Chances are you would tell someone before the person caused an accident, and you would feel justified because you did it on behalf of the inebriated person and his or her potential victim. But there seems to be a disconnect when it comes to bullying, which basically amounts to the same thing—someone who is drunk on power and control is victimizing an innocent person.

"While writing this paper, I discovered three new bullies that I had overlooked and never considered as bullies. The first is the sibling at home or that brother or sister who picks on, taunts, abuses, makes fun of, and takes advantage of another child in the family or home. They don't realize that they're conditioning their brother or sister to being bullied. They think it's okay, and even the parents dismiss it as sibling rivalry, but it's not okay. The act of bullying at home amounts to putting another boulder in the mental wagon of the victim. This is a wagon that they must pull throughout their life. At some point, there will be a breakdown. That breakdown could end up in the form of a suicide or a homicide, and I don't know which is worse. The second one is the system or world itself—the cultural times, the ACLU, the factions in society that are housed in government, or other institutions in Western civilization that uphold the rights of some while *choking* the rights of others. I heard recently from a cousin down in Georgia that a local school board there is trying to suspend or even expel students who are not meeting the academic standards, thereby denying kids the right to pursue an education that was paid for by taxpayers. That's just another form of bullying. With bullying inevitably comes victimization. This bully, the system, choke-holds the right of Christians in America to pray in public places or at school functions, and it even interferes with their right to recite the Pledge of Allegiance in the classroom. It causes the identity of Americans to change to the point that we no longer even remember the words of "The Star-Spangled Banner." This bully takes away the right of parents to discipline their children while giving the children the power to bully their parents. This bully militarizes police departments, giving them permission to shoot, choke, or beat the life out of citizens, thus creating an atmosphere of mistrust that could very well be inter-preted as an implied state of martial law. This creates a terrible division between law-enforcement personnel and the community they are sworn to protect. Now the members of the community are afraid of being killed by the police, while the police are afraid of being ambushed or assassinated by the members of the community. Maybe if we, as a nation, stood up together on May 4, 1970, at Kent State University—where Ohio National Guardsmen fired sixty-seven bullets in thirteen seconds, killing four unarmed college students and wounding nine others, one of whom suffered permanent paralysis—the national crisis of bullying wouldn't have made into high schools and middle schools. Problems are not self-correcting. What is a problem today will only become a crisis tomorrow if somebody doesn't do something. I read somewhere that "the only thing necessary for evil to triumph is for good men to do nothing," and I think that is very true. When David fought Goliath, the whole army of Israel was afraid to stand against one big bully, and it took a shepherd boy who was out of his league and in over his head to put a stop to it. By the way, he had been bullied by his older brothers for years—just as Joseph had been before he was thrown into a pit and sold into slavery. Sometimes our siblings can help us find the courage and strength we need to deal with our bullies in life because even life itself can be a bully. But there are times when our siblings join our bullies and we stand alone like a soldier without a country. In times like these, we Christians have to remember that Christ is the big brother who will give us the courage and strength to effectively deal with our bullies."

Gizzmoe reached into his pocket and pulled out an armband that he made that was of three col-ors—red, white, and blue. He placed it on his arm and continued talking. "Red symbolizes action, confidence, and courage. It means I will have the courage to take action against bullying with con-fidence although it may cost me a black eye or two, but that's a small price to pay and far less costly when I consider the pain of standing at the gravesite of a sibling, a classmate, or a teacher. White symbolizes purity, for the values of country, school, and family are pure and worth remembering and preserving. Finally, blue stands for all the bruises of the people who have been unjustly victimized by bullies—whether it is on the playground, in the hallway, in the home, or wherever. I have made enough for each of you. Please come down to the front, pick one up, put it on, and wear it for the rest of the week or even beyond."

Each member of the class collected one and wore it. Even his bully took one, and he later thanked Gizzmoe for opening his eyes and making him see things he never would've. Needless to say, Gizzmoe got an A that day. But he also got suspended for violating the school's dress code. And the only thing I can say to that is "What the heck—only in America!"

The End

The Bus Driver

Once there was a bus driver who was very thoughtful, caring, meticulous, and safe. She had seen many roads and had an ostentatious record. This day started out much like any other, but when she entered her bus, she noticed a child way in the back. The child was beautiful, and she seemed to possess something very special that the bus driver could not put her finger on. Attached to the child was a note that said, "Please get my child to where she's going." The bus driver was perplexed, for she did not know where the child was going, nor could the child tell her. The bus driver resigned from all her other activities and set out on a quest to discover the destination of the infant she instantly fell in love with. The driver became compelled with devotion and was dedicated to this little girl.

The two of them bonded in ways that cannot be spoken of, let alone written. They ate together, slept together, walked together, laughed together, and even cried together from time to time. The driver gave the child her all, and they traveled through life experiences almost as one. But as time went on and the child grew, something went somewhat awry. The bus driver's peace was disturbed, for she was forced to remember the note attached to the child, who now was almost grown. "Please get my child to where she's going." The driver had become so focused on the happiness, joy, and fulfillment that the child brought her that she chose to forget what she had purposed in her heart to do. The driver could sense the bond between them weakening as the emotional, psychological, and maybe even spiritual umbilical cord began to be severed. No matter what the driver did to eradicate the feeling and change the disturbance in her soul, the circumstance remained unchanged.

The driver had ceased to focus on the plea of the note and had become somewhat selfish. She did not want the child to leave her side. The driver had stopped asking herself what that note meant and had become caught up in the wonder and satisfaction of motherhood. She failed to remember that one day, the child would discover the note, for not only was it written on a piece of paper, but it was also in her subconscious and genetic code. The driver knew that the day would come when the child would leave to discover where she was going. The driver put on her sunglasses of denial and said to herself, "The day might come, but this is not the day," and she went about her life, focusing on the child while basking in the fulfillment, satisfaction, and joy the child brought her.

As the leaves began to turn, the driver awoke from a nap. She was about to go to the school to pick up the child, who was now a teenager, when she discovered a stranger, a man, sitting at her kitchen table. Before she could ask him who he was and how he got there, the man vanished before her eyes. Finally, she arrived at the school. After she managed to park behind other cars and thirty minutes before the school let the students out, the man appeared beside her, materializing in the passenger seat. Startled, she asked, "Who are you?"

He replied, "Zaphiel [the guardian angel of children]."

Zaphiel then began to speak to her. "I came for the child. Do you remember the day the child came into your life? There was a message that came with her. It asked you to get her to where she was going. I am here to explain to you the things you questioned and did not understand. Everyone living comes to this earthly plane by choice. The Heavenly Father allowed it in His permissive will for them to be born to you for a reason. The reason has to do with preparing them for their purpose as they ascend and transcend to the next level of their spiritual development. Your children are on loan to you, but they do not belong to you, for they belong to the Heavenly Father who created them. The message meant that your job is to help them grow and develop so they can reach their fullest potential while understanding that they are born with a purpose in life. Living is the process of discovering that purpose through trials, tribulations, experiences, tests, situations, and circumstances.

"A parent's role is not to possess a child but rather to prepare the child for the next level in life. Oftentimes, during the preparation process, a parent does not prepare himself or herself for the day when the swallow grows wings and flies away. God the Father gives us all something that He won't take back or let the devil take away, and that is our own free will to choose. In the normal course of development, babies grow up and become independent, leaving the nurturing, protective love of their parents and flying off to have their own ideas, decisions, families, and so forth. But such a departure leaves a hole in the heart of a mother, and mankind describes the hole in the phrase *empty-nest syndrome*. It's not necessarily a bad thing when mothers fulfill a part of who they are and are intended to be by loving, nurturing, and protecting their babies. But parents have to understand that they will cripple the growth and development of the child on loan to them when they do not allow them to move to the next stage or level of their development.

"Love can be selfish or unselfish and helpful or hurtful; thus, it can be good or bad. The child you found was a means that your Heavenly Father used to help you move to the next level. He blessed you with something you could love more than yourself. His intent was for you to embrace that, not possess that, for you cannot possess it any more than you can the song of a bird or the beauty of a rainbow. But you are a parent until one of you is called home although the parameters of the relationship might change. But it might help you to know that the bond of love surpasses your earthly existence, and neither death nor the grave can filter it, for the love the two of you share will be carried for all eternity. When I told you I came for the child, I did not mean that I came to take the child away. Rather, I came to act in the interest of the child, for you were about to destroy and cripple her with your love. Now that you understand what you did not before, I am free to leave."

And on that note, in the blink of an eye, Zaphiel disappeared. Suddenly, the child tugged at the car's door handle and hopped inside without taking a breath. She asked the bus driver when she was going to help her get her driver's license—something the driver had been putting off for quite some time. The bus driver now had a new outlook; her perception was humbling, reassuring, poised, and certain. She no longer feared losing the child, for she no longer saw her as something that she had to possess. She just looked at the child, and on the way home, she detoured to the state-patrol station and picked up a booklet for the rules of the road and the child's learner's permit. Yes, life changed for both the driver and the child that day. Ten years later, the driver became a grandma, and she rediscovered her purpose as she taught the child how to raise her own children. "Ah, how blessed I am to have had that divine visitation! Now I can be a mother all over again, but this time, I can take them home to their parents when they get on my nerves!"

The End

Hiding Out

It was getting close to the time when a group of souls would inhabit the bodies of unborn infants, and they were seated before Metatron (the angel that serves behind the throne of God and is referred to as His scribe) for one of a series of orientation classes that are centered on the act of being born. The souls were eager to be birthed into the world and had been taking classes to prepare for the journey. Metatron told them that he wanted to do something outside the box for this important lesson. A simple exercise in the form of a game would be the instructional tool he would use to inject the lesson for the day. "The game," he said, "is called hide-and-seek." Metatron took all the souls to Paradise and told them they were to hide while he counted to ten, and then he would try to find them. If they made it to the Tree of Life and touched it before he found them, then they would be home free. I cannot give you an accounting of all the souls who participated, but I will give you a few of the eventful and categorical hiding places they chose. Metatron leaned against the tree with his eyes resting on his forearm and started to count. The souls ran like roadrunners, heading toward different hiding places, and then the game was on.

One soul hid in his soon-to-be family, while another hid in the business he was going to have once he was born. One hid in a church choir, while another hid in his own self (i.e., his beauty, ego, talents, etc.). One hid in an affliction (e.g., cerebral palsy, blindness, deafness, lameness, etc.), while another hid in the clergy. One hid in sports (e.g., football, baseball, basketball, etc.), while another hid in the arts (e.g., dancing, acting, writing, etc.). One hid as a parent (e.g., present or absent, involved or uninvolved, abusive or nonabusive, Christian or atheist, etc.), while another hid as a child (e.g., delinquent or nondelinquent, high school graduate or dropout, loner or bully, advantaged or disadvantaged, etc.). One hid in a personality (e.g., controlling or empowering, positive or negative, inviting or discouraging, etc.), while another hid in a behavior (e.g., addictive or nonaddictive, promiscuous or faithful, etc.).

During the progress of the game, Heaven held an emergency meeting because mankind (via the new world order) had decided to circumvent God's plan to populate the earth by way of birth. The government passed laws that suspended traditional births, electing to clone human beings instead. Their rationale was that doing so would control the birth rate while redistributing global resources more effectively and ridding the planet of hunger, sickness, and war. Such a practice would have grave ramifications since clones would lack souls and thus would become vessels for the fallen. Consequently, Metatron called out to the souls, asking them to return to the class for the game had been suspended. Some of the souls could hear him, while others either could not hear him or would not respond to him. The souls that were willing returned, while the ones that were unwilling did not and therefore had to be found. This was not the first search-and-rescue mission Heaven had conducted. Long ago, there was one born via the Immaculate Conception who was named Emmanuel and was referred to as the Lion of Judah, the King of Kings, the Lord of Lords, and the Christ. He went to earth on a search-and-rescue mission that was ordered by the Father. He was to rescue Jews and Gentiles—the living and dead ones—from damnation single-handedly.

Some souls returned to the classroom located in the third Heaven, and when Metatron entered, he discovered many souls sharing their hiding-place experiences, clearly oblivious to the clone crisis. After calling the class to order, Metatron was confronted with several questions of the awaiting souls. The first was "What was the point of the exercise?" And the second was "Where are the other souls who have not returned?" Metatron was pleased to field both questions as they provided an easy intro into the lesson plan written by God Himself. Metatron answered them in this manner: "It is important for all of you to understand that you cannot hide from God, who is all-knowing, all-seeing, omnipotent, omniscient, and omnipresent. Notice that the hiding places you were allowed did not consist of trees, mountains, clouds, or anything of a physical nature; rather, they were things not defined by or composed of matter. Once you leave here and begin your journeys, you will go through a prodigal period. A prodigal period is a condition whereby you end up leaving the Father, striking out on your own. While you journey, you will be seduced by satanic IEDs that will be designed to prevent your return to Heaven. These devices range from religion to thought, from occupations to obsessions, and from real estate to rock and roll.

"There have been many in the past who tried to hide from or escape Almighty God. Saul, before he was anointed the first king of Israel, hid from God among the rubbish or baggage. Moses hid in the court of the Pharaoh. Jonah hid in the belly of the ship. Paul hid in his zealous persecution and execution of Christians. Nicodemus hid in the shadows of his status and profession. God still found them. You see, men still try to hide from God through many different, creative ways, thinking they can find sanctuary by camouflaging themselves. They hide in the rubbish of their jobs and professions, in sports, in crime, in money, or in property or even in the clergy and the church. Some hide in hatred, racism, party politics, church choirs, pulpits, religion, or marriage. No matter what you choose to hide in, God will know where you are and will find you, especially if He will choose you for a specific purpose. You must understand and never forget that you are born with a purpose and bought with a price.

"There are some who refuse to come after they've been called. This is the reason why many of the souls you started out with are not here right now. They were called but refused to come out of hiding because they are too comfortable in the comfort zones of their stuff. You must remember that the Almighty gives us all something that He won't take back or let the devil take away, and that is our own free will to choose. Unfortunately, there are those who choose not to be found, choose not to hear, choose not to believe, choose not to return, and choose not to be saved. Whatever may motivate such an act, it makes no difference. God doesn't leave you. Rather, you leave Him. He will never be the prodigal one. Each day of your existence is another opportunity to walk toward Him. If you do that, then you will come closer to your return and ending your prodigal period. Returning is a continuous process, and the objective is to grow closer to God and Christ each and every day. The bottom line is that many souls avoid God and attempt to hide within their stuff. The Word says that 'many are called but few are chosen.' If God chooses you, He will find you, and you will discover that your arms are just too short to box with God. Whenever He calls, you have the choice to answer or to continue hiding. Hiding always results in your demise. God wants you to succeed and not fail and to return to Him and not hide. Lastly, He wants you to be saved and not lost. Be blessed!"

The End

The Tour

A grandfather thought it would be important to take his grandkids on an important, thought-provoking, insightful, and (hopefully) life-changing tour. Bear in mind that his numerous children live in different states and various parts of the world. He had many grandchildren as well. So the grandfather arranged for all the grandkids to come during a time when they all could share the planned experience he had contemplated in his heart. Finally, the day came for the tour. The children expected to go to the zoo, the aquarium, or maybe even a theme park, but instead, he took them to a hospital. He strolled them through the intensive care unit, where they saw people lying in comas and hooked up to all kinds of breathing apparatuses. Then they went down to the nursery to see the newborns, and this was followed by a trip to the emergency room. Finally, they went to the morgue. After they left the hospital, the grandfather took them to a park and found a weeping willow near a pond and began to talk to them all while they enjoyed their ice creams.

While he spent quality time with them, one of the children asked him why he took them to the hospital rather than a zoo, an aquarium, a theme park, or even a movie. The grandfather smiled and began his talk. "You see, when God breathed the breath of life into Adam and he became a living soul, having been made in the image and likeness of God, Adam became conscious. He was awakened to a knowledge of 'self' and his surroundings. He detected the presence of something other than himself and his environment, and that something was Almighty God. Thus, Adam had become God-conscious. When we are entirely conscious, we are *fully aware* and not partially aware. Whenever we are alive but not conscious, then we are in a state of sleep. Whenever the sleep state persists for longer than a specified period of time, then one enters a coma or comatose state, which is nothing more than a prolonged state of unconsciousness. That means that they lack the ability to respond to stimuli, and it becomes almost impossible to rouse or wake them. One can be awake and still not be aware. One can be aware yet not fully conscious. When a person is partially aware and has difficulty with their balance or detecting their surroundings and cannot even determine the time or what they are doing, then they are said to be in an altered state of consciousness. Intoxicants such as drugs and alcohol are known to produce altered states of consciousness. There are three states of altered consciousness—obtundation, drowsiness, and stupor. To be obtunded is to be dull, blunt, or deadened. To be stuporous is to be in an apathetical suspension, like the effect caused by narcotics or alcohol. And when we are drowsy, we are half-asleep and half-awake. These three conditions or states of consciousness exist between the two extremes of consciousness, which are fully wake and brain-dead' Consciousness is always related to awareness and responsiveness in respect to some stimulus. A stimulus is something that incites an action or exertion or quickens an action, feeling, or thought or causes something to function or operate. An example would be defibrillation. Defibrillation consists of delivering a therapeutic dose of electrical energy to the heart with a device called a defibrillator in order to reestablish a heartbeat. Spiritual stimuli are experiences, situations, circumstances, tragedies, traumas, encounters, and so forth. Comas can be physical and can be spiritual as well.

"Many of us exist in a state of spiritual obtundation. Many of us can be spiritually drowsy, be in a kind of spiritual stupor, or even in spiritual comas because we are not fully aware of the presence, power, acts, words, and will of God in everything. Therefore, we are not God-conscious. Jesus was God-conscious because he was fully aware of the presence, power, acts, words, and will of God in everything! Yeshua was with God the Father and the Holy Spirit before the earth was created. But before we can ever become God-conscious, we must first become Christ-conscious, for Jesus said, 'No one cometh unto the Father but by me.' Also, we need to be conscious of the Comforter—the Holy Spirit. Now let's take a closer look at what we observed in the hospital and what it symbolically means to us spiritually. To begin with, we need to understand that the church is like the hospital in that it is the place where sick, unconscious, half-asleep, stuporous, obtunded, or comatose souls go to seek God. There is an old saying: 'The church was not intended to be a hotel for saints but rather a hospital for sinners, and all have sinned and come short of the glory of God.'

"Those of us who refuse to acknowledge the presence of God in creation and who are not aware of His Word, acts, will, and intervention in our lives are in spiritual comas because we do not respond to the external stimulus of His voice whenever He tries to get our attention through situations or circumstances in order to show us something He wants us to know, learn, or understand. We are thus spiritually brain-dead. The Bible refers to this as being reprobate. When we are reprobate, it is impossible for us to hear God and respond to His stimuli, and we, therefore, can no longer function spiritually. When we enter spiritual comas, nothing seems to go right for us, we can't seem to prosper, we always seem to be sick, and nothing seems to make us happy. We end up existing—surviving life rather than living and enjoying it. We end up thinking what is wrong is right and what is right is wrong through justification. We also begin to place more importance on what is acceptable to man than what is acceptable to Almighty God, thus worshipping the creature more than the Creator. Romans 1:18–32 [KJV] states, 'For the wrath of God is revealed from heaven against all ungodliness and unrighteousness of men, who hold the truth in unrighteousness; Because that which may be known of God is manifest in them; for God hath shewed it unto them. For the invisible things of him from the creation of the world are clearly seen, being understood by the things that are made, even his eternal power and Godhead; so that they are without excuse: Because that, when they knew God, they glorified him not as God, neither were thankful; but became vain in their imaginations, and their foolish heart was darkened. Professing themselves to be wise, they became fools, And changed the glory of the uncorruptible God into an image made like to corruptible man, and to birds, and fourfooted beasts, and creeping things. Wherefore God also gave them up to uncleanness through the lusts of their own hearts, to dishonour their own bodies between themselves: Who changed the truth of God into a lie, and worshipped and served the creature more than the Creator, who is blessed for ever. Amen For this cause God gave them up unto vile affections: for even their women did change the natural use into that which is against nature: And likewise also the men, leaving the natural use of the woman, burned in their lust one toward another; men with men working that which is unseemly, and receiving in themselves that recompence of their error which was meet. And even as they did not like to retain God in their knowledge, God gave them over to a reprobate mind, to do those things which are not convenient; Being filled with all unrighteousness, fornication, wickedness, covetousness, maliciousness; full of envy, murder, debate, deceit, malignity; whisperers, Backbiters, haters of God, despiteful, proud, boasters, inventors of evil things, disobedient to parents, Without understanding, covenantbreakers, without natural affection, implacable, unmerciful: Who knowing the judgment of God, that they which commit such things are worthy of death, not only do the same, but have pleasure in them that do them.'

"Now the nursery is the place for newborns—those souls who have accepted that Jesus is the Christ and have given their hearts and lives over to him—or babes in Christ who have recently been born again. Their slates are blank and are to be written upon with the acts of their own wills in respect to the Word and the will of God the Father. The nurses in the ward are like the guardian angels God has assigned to care for and protect us around the clock. Like newborn babies, they depend on their spiritual family and parents to feed and nurture them until they can become self-sufficient in the Word and the ways of God and Christ. Sometimes they soil themselves, and the Holy Spirit has to change the diapers of their hearts, minds, and attitudes. Always remember, children, that before anything will change on the outside, something first must change on the inside. There can never be a permanent change in behavior unless there first is a change in attitude. Like all newborns, spiritual infants have to learn how to talk, walk, eat, and put on their clothes in order to grow and develop properly.

"Now let's talk about what we saw in the emergency room. First of all, an emergency room is a hospital area that is equipped to provide the prompt treatments for acute illnesses, traumas, or other medical emergencies. Depending on the extent of the malady, one might receive treatment and then go back home, or they might have to be admitted and require a longer time for treatment or recovery. We saw every kind of victim—from gunshot to car-wreck, from flu to infection, from blood-pressure to stroke, and from alcohol-poisoning and drug-overdose to allergic reaction to the wrong medication. We saw all ages, all sexes, all races, all occupations, as well as the rich and the poor. We saw the spectrum of humanity, and none were exempt. Spiritually speaking, many of us become traumatized by death, sickness, accident, and loss. Whether it be the loss of a loved one or the loss of a job or a home, it makes no difference. If we're not careful, we can become infected by false doctrines or by hanging out with the wrong crowd. Truly, association does bring about assimilation over time. These things occur when we live like we're spiritually asleep or in a spiritual stupor. And if we're not really careful, we can end up SDOA—spiritually dead on arrival. We will then be taken to the morgue, for we will not recover unless Christ himself resurrects us as he did Lazarus. All of you must realize, understand, and remember to be God-conscious as you aspire to become the men and women God has purposed for you to be. And if you happen to forget, ask the Holy Spirit to remind you and seek Christ to help you, and He will. Doing so will make both God and Grandpa happy and proud.

"In conclusion, if it's been a long time since you've been roused by the Word or an anointed sermon, then you just might be in a spiritual coma or some state of altered spiritual consciousness. You might be in a spiritual stupor or obtunded. You may have become spiritually intoxicated and contaminated by false doctrines, wrong associations, wrong interpretations of the Word, or wrong responses to everyday situations and circumstances. It is incumbent upon us all to check ourselves before we wreck ourselves. We must ask God to create in us a clean heart and renew in us a right spirit. David said in the Psalm 139, 'Search me oh God and know my heart, try me and know my thoughts and see if there be any wicked way in me and lead me in the way everlasting.' Now, children, enjoy your ice cream, and may God take a liking to you all."

The End

The Alcoholic Helper

(Based on a True Story)

Once there was a time when Itsunme, as a young man, hated alcoholics. Having been born and reared in a small southern mountain town where moonshine ruled and was king, he had always been around people who drank to escape the pains of everyday life and lived for the weekend. The population of the small town was around eighteen thousand, and the residents were hardworking, proud, independent hillbillies. It's important to understand the culture of that time. Every year, as far back as he could remember, an alcoholic in his community died each winter by falling down drunk on the way home at night from some bootlegger's house and then freezing to death. In the fall, he would wonder who it would be that year. Needless to say, it was not uncommon for temperatures to plunge below freezing. The town was in a "dry county," which meant that it was against the law to make or sell alcohol there. But this rule only made liquor houses realize enormous profits from the sale of the illegal liquid, especially late at night.

What made it worse was he saw so many of his friends' lives destroyed by the substance. His parents had been alcoholics before they found the Lord. But his uncle (his daddy's brother) was always drunk, as was his wife. His uncle loved him dearly; he hugged him every time he saw him. But the smell of alcohol emanating from the pores of his skin like the odor of roadkill baking in the hot southern sun made him nauseous and repulsed. There was never a time he wasn't sickened by the disgusting smell, but he never acted as though it bothered him because of the love and respect he felt for his daddy's only brother. But worse than that, their children (his cousins) suffered atrociously from the hell-spun liquid in ways unimaginable. His uncle and aunt fought all the time, chasing each other with butcher knives and axes and traumatizing him and their children. The residents of the town worked the mills during the week, but when the weekend came, they would let their hair down by drinking to escape the pains of poverty. He was amazed how men working on the backs of the city's trash trucks could hang on with one hand, like Indiana Jones on some crusade, while being drunk as a skunk or Cooter Brown, as the old folks would often say. One was named J-Bird, another was named Sparrow, and a third was named Logg. Logg bore a scar from ear to ear where Itsunme's dad had literally cut Logg's throat for getting fresh with his mom thirty years prior.

Itsunme remembered that when he was seven, the parents of two of his classmates fought on the dirt road in front of his house. He shook and trembled now just like he did then when the husband (a known drinker) stopped their car and got out with his pocketknife drawn to cut his wife, who was running for her life around the car and calling for help while throwing big rocks through the windshield. While revisiting the trauma in his mind, he wondered if the same scenario would have occurred if there had been no alcohol. Both bore scars from the times they had carved each other up over the years before Itsunme was born. His older brother, who is older than him by nineteen months, started drinking when he was only fourteen years old and is an alcoholic to this very day. The town's cemeteries were littered with the graves of perpetrators and victims who died on account of driving under the influence. I could tell you countless stories Itsunme shared with me about all the wrecks that happened up there in hairpin turns or railroad tracks or even about the ones that went off the side of the mountain, but time will not allow me to do so; therefore, I'll just get right to the main point.

In 1981, he was living in the hood in Atlanta. He was working at Hayes Microcomputer Products while going to GA Tech and Atlanta Junior College simultaneously. He had met a young lady, Renee, who captured his fancy, and she lived in the projects behind him—Carver Homes, to be exact. It was on a Sunday evening when he decided to visit her after church. The street she lived on was a one-way one, and there was no room to park on the road. Deciding to pull up onto the grass beyond the sidewalk, he maneuvered his vehicle off the street so other cars could get by. But while driving onto the sidewalk, he did not notice that a manhole cover was off, and his left rear wheel (the pulling wheel) went down the hole. Bear in mind that he had paid his rent, utilities, and child support. He placed his last twenty dollars into the collection plate at church thirty minutes prior and was broke. He tried to get out of the hole, but the smell of burning rubber further discouraged him. His ability to get to work the next day was paramount, but he had nothing left; he could not even call a tow truck, and the small automobile-insurance company that the town had did not provide roadside service. Under his breath, he called on the Lord, and no sooner had he finished calling than he heard the words of a drunk alcoholic. "You stuck, ain't you?"

This aggravated Itsunme; he really disliked alcoholics then. Very rudely and disrespectfully he replied, "Yeah. So what?"

The drunk said, "I can get dat car out dat hole. You got a jack?"

Itsunme opened his trunk desperately and pulled the jack out. After spotting the jack and without another word, the drunk got up from the wooden straight-backed chair he was sitting in and made his way toward the car. He stumbled and fell two feet off the back porch he had been sitting on. This reminded Itsunme of the many drunks he had seen in his lifetime, but he said nothing. Before the man traveled the twenty to twenty-five feet necessary to reach the vehicle, he fell at least two more times. The old guy jacked the car (a green 1977 Chevy Malibu) up; the back wheel was now a foot higher than the hole. Turning to Itsunme, he said, "Now get in. Crank it up. And when I tell you, you step on it."

Itsunme did as he was instructed. The old drunk started to rock the car gently back and forth, and on the third rock, he said "Hit it!" as he pushed the car forward with all his might and then crashed to the ground in a drunken stupor. The car lunged ahead with the pulling wheel hitting the front edge of the hole, gaining traction, and lunging onto the grass safely. In his rearview mirror, Itsunme saw the jack pop out and fly thirty feet behind him, missing the alcoholic by six inches.

The car was out. The man was safe, and God had done more than simply answer his prayer, for he learned a valuable lesson as well. He helped the old man up, thanked him, and helped him get back to the chair on his back porch. No sooner had he gotten back into the driver's seat than the Spirit of the Lord fell upon him and spoke to him about the experience. In silent whispers, God chastised him about judging people, especially alcoholics. He said to Itsunme that He had not called us to judge one another but rather to *love* one another. He made Itsunme realize that none of the church folk had even stopped to offer him assistance, and the only Samaritan who cared about his plight was the old drunk. That old drunk had more compassion and Christ than all the choir-singing, usher-bearing, deacon-praying Christians he had thought so highly of. God had used the one he least expected to help him, to save him, and yes, to teach him. Itsunme did not know if the man was an angel in disguise or merely a man who knew God but was struggling with an issue in his life. He came to realize that we all struggle with something and maybe if we knew more about a person, their history, and their past experiences, we might better understand why they do what they do. But Christ could and did. Perhaps that's why he did not condemn the woman at the well, the beggars at the gates, the man possessed by legions, or you or me. Maybe that's why He said, "Judge ye not" and "Love one another as I have loved you." He knew that it's love that brings us back, not condemnation.

Itsunme then felt bad about all the times his uncle had hugged him and he grimaced rather than hug him back. From now on, he would not resist giving change to the winos or homeless people asking for quarters or spare change. He realized the opportunity to be blessed that one gains when one gives without judging, leaving what is done with the money up to the person and God. He realized that the only difference between him and the addict, the alcoholic, the homeless, the convict, or the chronically unemployed is simply the grace of God. He came to know the power that comes from not judging and the blessing that comes from asking God to protect and deliver a person from the attacks of Satan and his host. He came to see and understand that sometimes people are so bound that they can't even pray for themselves and need others to stand in the gap for them. He helped me understand that loving a person cannot be achieved when one imposes one's will, dreams, standards, or values on them. Only God can change a person, and He alone can teach us how to rightly love them. Maybe they are there to help us see ourselves and evaluate the Christ in us that we think we have. Perhaps it's not as much as we reckoned. Nonetheless, his story was edifying, uplifting, and enlightening to me, and it changed the way I view my fellow men. I can only hope and pray that it has done the same for you.

The End

The Jar

Dear Dr. Phil,

I'm writing you this letter and pleading for your help because I've seen you on TV and observed how helpful you can be to those suffering and in need. The truth is that I'm having an identity crisis. It all started one day when someone put a candle in me, but the candle wasn't enough; I needed something more. No, it's nothing like that. I'm not talking about anything sexual or freaky. You see, I am a mason jar, and I was born in 1858—when John Landis Mason invented and patented a way to can or preserve food. The Ball Company bought him out around 1909. But let me get back to the point. I was created to hold things of substance—things that have meaning or importance. When I held the candle, it was the most important day of my life, for I contained and emanated light and heat. Everybody and everything around me looked up to me for the first time. Whenever I held vegetables or meat, I felt important too, but not in the same way I did when I surrounded the candle. Even though holding food was important, I still felt unappreciated. But when the light shined in me for the first time, I had a greater sense of purpose and meaning that somehow seemed to change my identity. Suddenly, I held brilliance and warmth—things that one cannot eat, hold in the hand, or even ignore. For the first time since my creation, I had a sense of importance and was admired by other items that rested on the shelf where I sat. In short, not only was I revered and looked up to, but I was also admired, envied, and valued more than I had previously been.

Having the candle inside me was truly a euphoric experience, and everything was fine for a while, but then one of the people living in this house screwed my lid on tight, and from that time on, nothing was the same. All the air was sealed outside of me, and the air that was left inside burned up quickly, causing the candle to go out. As the light and warmth disappeared, the admiration, appreciation, purpose, meaning, reverence, brilliance, and envy I had obtained left also, and if that wasn't enough, my new identity was gone as well.

I remember when Madge and Zack first bought me in the late 1970s. They were hippies in their younger days, but after getting married and maturing a bit, they started to take life more seriously and responsibly. They bought a house and started raising kids.

They were naturalists and very health-conscious, so Madge decided to stay as far away from preservatives, insecticides, and pesticides as she possibly could, especially when it came to food. She was from West Virginia, and Zack hailed from Tres Lagunas, New Mexico, near the Pecos Wilderness, somewhere close to Pie Town, New Mexico. Needless to say, both knew and loved the benefits of living off the land. Having been the mother of nine children, Madge's mother was a master canner, so after Madge had three kids of her own, she decided to accept the torch her mother was passing, preserving the values, traditions, and ways inherent in the West Virginia mountains (with the exception of feuding, of course). Zack—an avid vegetable gardener, hunter, and fisherman—was a bit of a survivalist. He didn't trust the government and large corporations; therefore, he only believed in going to the grocery store for flour, sugar, salt, pepper, and other staple goods. Madge finally got the hang of canning and used me for putting up (preserving) everything from green beans to groundhogs year after year; however, as the years went by, Tupperware, plastic containers, ziplock bags, deep freezers, and frozen foods appealed to Madge. They made food preservation more convenient while saving her time. When those things came about and took over, my usefulness waned.

I got excited one day when one of the children unscrewed my lid. Suddenly, there was a rush like you wouldn't believe. The empty vacuum was at last ended, but to my dismay, what went inside me was not what I wanted or expected. Warmth ensued, but it was not from a candle; rather, it was from the heat generated by habanero peppers. The disappointment was devastating. I wanted—no, craved the warmth and light the candle brought. All the objects in the room, including the other containers on the shelf where I sat, laughed at me. One of them even called me a Ball Jar. I thought I was escaping their ridicule when someone removed me from the shelf and took me into their room, but he only wanted to have me hold many things for about six months. The things he placed in me were heroin, marijuana, moonshine, rubbing alcohol, syringes, cotton balls, Q-tips, and soil. I am the only mason jar left out of the twelve that were bought. The others that were in the box with me perished from breakage inside the dishwasher and being knocked off the table, but I somehow survived without even a chip. Now I wonder if it might have been better if I had suffered their fate, for now my purpose has been abandoned, and my identity and my self-respect have been lost. I need your help, for my sanity is slipping away. I am at a loss and cannot make sense of it all. The only good thing that happened is I was placed back on the shelf where I sat for years.

No sooner had I finished the letter than I got my answer, but it wasn't from Dr. Phil. Instead, it was coming from the room where I resided. After calling me by my name, he began his dissertation.

"Mason, you and I have a lot in common. Although we're different, we're still the same, for we are both containers. Dr. Phil may or may not be able to help you, but I can. You see, what you have gone through and are going through is symbolic of people's lives." Oftentimes, the people's current condition or circumstance causes them to quest for temporary happiness and pleasure as opposed to a more elevated state of consciousness that would bring true fulfillment. Living according to an elevated consciousness will cause people to concentrate more on what they accomplish with their lives as opposed to how much they are able to accumulate in them. Whenever these superficial and temporary gratification systems fail, people find themselves sealed off in a virtual vacuum where nobody seems to see, understand, or care about them; they begin to feel just as you did when your candle burned out and the light went out. But then something in life screws their lids off, and their vacuums are filled with things that rush in, consuming their very souls, characters, and identities. This makes them blind, leaving them unable to see who they are for they can only remember the vision of who they once were. Many times people blame others for what they allow to fill the vacuums within their souls—things like hatred, racism, drugs, materialism, hopelessness, etc. Whenever that happened, *you ceased to be a jar and became an unspecified container.*

But if we empty ourselves of the garbage (hatred, racism, drugs, materialism, pessimism, hopelessness, etc.) that we have allowed to fill us, then we will create a space whereby someone or something can come along and place another candle (the symbol of enlightenment) inside us, making us mason jars (which symbolize a purpose-filled life with an identity) once again instead of aimless, unspecified containers (life loiterers who lack purpose or fulfillment). That candle will represent spirituality, optimism, hope, purpose, and the understanding that we are our brothers' keepers. Almost always that job is too big, complex, and complicated for the individual and an outside helpful force is required to remove the garbage. The Word of God is that outside helpful force, and Christ is the hand that will wash out your jar and sterilize your soul. If you allow Christ and the Holy Spirit to pump out the garbage in your heart, mind, soul, situation, circumstance, and all the other facets of your life, another more eternal candle will be placed inside your jar, and it will give you light, warmth, prosperity, peace, power, respect, and admiration. Others will tell the difference, and God will notice you in ways you cannot imagine, for 1 Corinthians 2:9 says, "But as it is written, Eye hath not seen, nor ear heard, neither have entered into the heart of man, the things which God hath prepared for them that love him." Philippians 3:10–14 says, "That I may know him, and the power of his resurrection, and the fellowship of his sufferings, being made conformable unto his death; If by any means I might attain unto the resurrection of the dead. Not as though I had already attained, either were already perfect: but I follow after, if that I may apprehend that for which also I am apprehended of Christ Jesus. Brethren, I count not myself to have apprehended: but this one thing I do, forgetting those things which are behind, and reaching forth unto those things which are before, I press toward the mark for the prize of the high calling of God in Christ Jesus. If you'll do that, then I guarantee you that you won't need to write to Dr. Phil or need to be filled with anything other than the *love and light of God!*"

The End

(Based on a True Story)

There's only one place in the whole world where Paul Anderson (once the strongest man on the planet), James Brown, Bobby Byrd, an NFL player for the New Orleans Saints (Patrick Swilling), an NBA player for the Indiana Pacers (Dale Davis), the top aide for Senator Sam Nunn (Thomas Dortch), and the only black man from northeastern Georgia to become a state-prison warden (Frederick Steeple) all hailed from, and if you know where that is, then you know where this story begins but not ends. It was late August, and Baby Boy was hitching a ride back to GA Tech after his wife left him stranded due to an argument that should never have taken place. He was angry, to say the least, but he had to get back to the married-student housing on North Avenue at all costs. Gwen and Tameesha (his wife and six-month-old baby girl) were already there, and it *seemed like* he had been walking for days. Finally, a tractor-trailer driver picked him up, and as he jumped into the cab, sweat poured down his head, face, and neck. After thanking the driver for stopping and then telling him how far he was going, Baby Boy closed his eyes in relief and to thank God for answering his prayer. Along the way, he began to remember events in his life that would become life-changing and character-forming. I think it was the season, the time of the year, the month, or maybe even the heat that triggered the memory of when he was starting school for the first time and was in need of school clothes and shoes. His mom, a presser and production worker at Wrights Manufacturing Company, wanted to take him into town so they could shop for Levis, long-sleeve shirts, and a pair of Buster Browns. Since he was the baby of the family, she could've just altered hand-me-downs from his older brother, but she chose not to; that was suitable when it came to playclothes but not for this occasion.

School was important to his family, for his daddy only reached the second grade. He had to leave school at age 7 when his mother died and therefore could not read or write, but he at least managed to learn how to sign his name. His mom reached the sixth grade when her daddy died, and she, along with her other brothers and sisters, had to leave school to work in order to save the farm, so she could only read and write a little more than his dad. He was excited that Saturday morning, standing up on the floorboard of his parents' 1956 turquoise and white Chevrolet Bel Air. He always held on to the cloth-covered, retractable rope that ran across the back of the front seat. It served as a kind of seat belt for that period. His mother was fast in everything she did, including driving. She had a lead foot and only knew two speeds—zero miles per hour and one hundred miles per hour.

Starting the first grade was a type of rite of passage because now he could truly be one of the boys. His older brother, Freddy, and their neighbors—Richard Dortch and his younger brother, Thomas "Tommy" Dortch—went to school. It *seemed like* everybody did but him. As his mother backed out of the driveway, Richard was walking down the street. Baby Boy was so happy, and he excitedly waved at his older friend and neighbor.

Once he broke his arm in three places after he got inside a car tire like Stymie of *The Little Rascals* and his cousin Emory Thornton rolled him down the hill from his grandmother's house on Sage Street toward M. C. Scott's house. The tire left the road, went down an embankment by the creek, and landed on his arm after ejecting him. His mother and her sister Martha (who also worked at Wrights as a presser) had gone to his grandmother's for lunch; upon seeing him hurt and suffering, she quickly swooped him up, threw him in the back of their car, and rocketed up the street to get to Dr. McNeely's. There were only two doctors in the town who would even touch black people at the time, Dr. Graves and Dr. McNeely, and Dr. McNeely was the closer one. He would always remember how that car left the ground and became airborne when she hit that hump. That was the first time his stomach went up to his mouth and would become his first theme park ride without a theme park. It *seemed like* the car wasn't going to touch down again. A lot of black women went to hairdressers in the hood (e.g., Mary Steeple, Julia Brown, Edith Wheeler) to get their hair straightened, but all they had to do was take a ride with Baby Boy's mother when she was in a hurry, and I guarantee you their hair would be straight by the time she stopped that car. His momma was like shooting a cheap pistol in that she was too hot to trot. She was smart, fast, adventurous, attractive, fashionable, ingenious, cutting-edge, and scared of nothing—not even his daddy!

When they got into town, they first went to Belk Gallants, where Mrs. Nobie Neal worked as a handywoman; she was the only black person in the whole store, and it was the only store in the whole town that employed a black. Now they were at the part that Baby Boy hated, which was trying everything on to see how it fit and looked on him. This went on for hours because she was buying a whole school wardrobe, not just an outfit or two. His mother was a value-conscious lady who conducted a cost-versus-benefit analysis in her head before making a purchase. That meant they had to go from Belk's to Nickleback's Shoe Store in order to compare the styles and prices of a pair of Buster Browns (everyday school shoes) and PF Flyers (tennis shoes). Lastly, they went to Harper's store for pencils, crayons, and Blue Horse writing tablets, which were the iPads of the 1950s. It *seemed like* it would never end.

Well, back to the story. Opening his eyes, he read something that said Lula, Georgia, and suddenly, he remembered that Joseph Buffington, also known as Tripp Monster, was from there. Billy Stanley, an architect major who felt it was his solemn duty to nickname all the incoming black students at GA Tech, had given Joseph that nickname, but only Billy could tell you why he chose Tripp Monster. But Billy did more than simply nickname; he had given Baby Boy advice on how to survive GA Tech's culture. Billy was like the Moses of GA Tech. He tried to help minority students succeed and matriculate. Those who listened to him and took his advice reached the promised land, and those who didn't ended up back in Egypt.

Closing his eyes once again, he remembered when he, his brother, his first cousin, and six other blacks joined the integrated public schools in Stephens County. He recalled how he had to literally fight to get in and fight to get out during the first two years. The memory of being treated like a leper at school was like swallowing his own vomit for a second time. The discrimination didn't *seem like* it would ever end, for most of the trailblazing black students at Tech got egged at least once by white students while they were on their way to class. He recalled how his high school guidance counselor, Ms. Tomlin, called him to her office while he was in chorus and told him, "You will never get accepted and go to GA Tech, and even if you do, you won't last three months." Ms. Vera Campbell, the teacher of the chorus class, was one of the five teachers (the rest were Ms. Perkins, Ms. Sims, Mr. Joe Vaughn, and Ms. Andrews) in the school who treated blacks with fairness, dignity, and respect. But God always has the final word on *seemed-like* situations. And he became the second black person in the history of northeastern Georgia to attend the Georgia Institute of Technology. Ben "The Raven" Davis was the first one.

"Been thumbing for a long time"? the driver asked.

"Longer than I would've liked to," replied Baby Boy.

"I didn't know they even had any blacks going to GA Tech. You're the first black boy I've met who goes there. Was it hard to get in?" the driver asked.

How long it took Baby Boy to answer is unknown, for his mind flashed back to the time after he graduated high school. He worked all summer long at the Six Flags in Georgia. He worked from 10:00 a.m. to 10:00 p.m. seven days a week to earn the money he needed to get himself in Albany State College. He had no help from the guidance office or Ms. Tomlin when he applied for admission or financial aid. But he resolved not to work in a factory in his hometown or become either an alcoholic or a teenage father. He sent off his fees by way of money order, keeping the receipts, and now the time had come to start his postsecondary education. His father hired a family friend, Murray Cochran (who was a fellow deacon and church member), to drive them—Baby Boy, his dad, and his brother—to Albany, Georgia. Upon their arrival, they found the dormitory where Baby Boy would be staying, and with bags in hand, they went in only to discover that a mistake had been made; too many had been admitted in respect to the number of rooms and beds available. Cots were scattered throughout the hallways, and the dorm manager told them that they did not see Baby Boy's name on the list. Baby Boy showed the man his receipt and the letter the school had sent to welcome him, but they were of no consequence. Baby Boy objected emphatically, but his father made him get back in the car, and they drove back home. Along the way, Baby Boy thought of all he'd been through beneath the Sunday coat over his head that prevented everyone else from seeing the tears that cascaded down his face. It *seemed like* all was lost and his sacrifices had been for naught. When he entered the house, his mother met him, wanting to know what happened, but he quickly pushed past her and ran into his room, closing the door without slamming it. He could hear his dad explaining to his mother the chain of events that led them back home, and Baby Boy was not pleased, but he was not defeated too, for he knew God. He was capable of parting the Red Sea when the children of Israel left Egypt. He shut the jaws of the lions when Daniel was in the den. He stuck by Joseph when he was sold into slavery and cast into prison for refusing to sleep with his master's wife. He knew that God ordered the ravens to bring meat and bread to Elijah when he was held up in a cave and knew that God helped David slay the giant Goliath with only one smooth stone. Perhaps He would smile upon him too and help Baby Boy cross over into his promised land. Down on his knees, he called upon God and found him. When he got up, he opened the door with his bags in his hands and asked his dad to take him to the Greyhound Bus station. His dad objected, telling him that they had no family or friends there and they did not know a place where he could stay. But Baby Boy was insistent, and he told his father that he had come too far, had worked too hard, and had suffered too much to quit now. So his dad reluctantly put him on the bus that evening.

He arrived in Atlanta between 8:00 to 8:30 p.m. and changed buses. He left Atlanta at around 11:00 p.m., heading for Albany. He met a lovely young lady who was of his age. She was named Alice Baisden, and her nickname was Cookie. The two of them talked and flirted the whole way and all night long. She got off the bus about an hour before it got to Albany, and that was the only time he slept in the last twenty-four hours. He exited the bus and was walking around the bus station when he met a guy by the name of George E. Cooper and his cousin Johnny from Darien, Georgia. The two guys were also freshmen at Albany State, and the three of them had a slice of pecan pie (Baby Boy's first) as they chitchatted about the school and what was going on. They later became like brothers, for George was staying with an old lady named Ms. Page, and he offered to ask her if Baby Boy could stay there too. So off they went to Ms. Page's, taking turns with carrying Baby Boy's huge suitcase. George said there was only one full-size bed there, and the two of them agreed to draw am imaginary line down the middle of it, and each guy vowed to stay on his side. Baby Boy was not only very smart or intelligent, but he was also a very sharp dresser and had the gift of gab. George and Johnny nicknamed him Pimp, and due to that, only 10 percent of the people on campus knew him by his real name, including Joel Bone from Elberton, Georgia, who became the fourth musketeer of the group. It wasn't long before Baby Boy was tutoring football players in math and swimming on the swim team with his friend Kenneth Cox. Needless to say, all the fraternities were trying to get him to pledge, while the ladies adored him. It *seemed like* Baby Boy's life had turned the corner from the outside, but inside was a different matter. Albany State was like a repeat of the ninth grade for him as he *never* studied and had a 4.0 GPA. He knew that would eventually cost him as he needed to be challenged, and the quest for GA Tech remained. At the end of the first quarter, the school closed for Christmas break, and Baby Boy journeyed to GA Tech to meet with Dr. Fran Roper (the registrar) to discover why he had not received a response to his application. Dr. Roper stated that he could not find the exact reason since Baby Boy had both the grades and the SAT scores required for admission. Dr. Roper said that GA Tech had a quota system and they only let a certain number of blacks in regardless of grades or SAT scores, but Baby Boy was insistent. He was so insistent that Dr. Roper saw his determination and made a deal with Baby Boy.

He said, "I will admit you under one condition, and that is under academic probation. You have one quarter to sink or swim, but it's too late for you to register for the winter quarter, so you'll have to enter in the spring quarter!"

Baby Boy shook his hand and stated, "I believe in the song James Brown sang. 'I don't want nobody to give me nothing. Just open up the door, and I'll get it myself.'"

Dr. Roper just smiled, and a week later, Baby Boy received his acceptance letter at his sister and brother-in-law's house. It was the school his sister prophesized he would go to when he was only ten years old—when there was no hint of a Civil Rights Bill.

It *seemed like* he would not get into college. It *seemed like* he would have no place to stay. It *seemed like* he would never go to GA Tech. It *seemed like* he was defeated, and all was lost. It *seemed like* he was drowning in disappointments and hardships that were brought on by situations and circumstances. It *seemed like* God wasn't listening and had forgotten him, but like Joseph, Baby Boy continued to trust God, refusing to give up or daring to disbelieve His Word, for He said, "I will never leave you nor forsake you," "Whatsoever you ask in prayer, believing, you shall receive," "I will not deny you any good thing," and "I can do all things through Christ who strengthens me."

"We're here," said the truck driver. "By the way, my name is George."

"I'm Baby Boy," replied the hitchhiker, and as he walked up the steep, grassy hill near the I-85, he said to himself, "Hmm, not another George!"

As far as what happened after he got home, well, that's a story I'm saving for a rainy day. You see, you can't pay attention to the *seemed like* because it's Satan's way of keeping you from experiencing the saving grace in God's Word, thus robbing you of His blessings as you sink like Peter when he tried to walk on water. God will show up in your circumstance if you trust Him and remember His promises. One thing's for sure—whenever He shows up, He also shows out because He exceeds what we might think or ask! This story is written for all the people experiencing the *seemed like.* For some people, it seems like they're not going to graduate, or they're not going to get well. For some, it might be that they feel they're not going to get another chance in life—that they're never going to have a child, get a car, find a mate, get out of debt, or get off probation. It could be that you feel you're not going to get paroled or maybe regain custody of your kids. It might *seem like* you're not going to get past a breakup or get out of the hospital or the jail/prison/solitary confinement or even death row, but just march around your situation with the Word of God like they marched around the walls of Jericho. Remember this story, and I guarantee you that like the Red Sea, your circumstance will part. The Goliath of your story will fall, and *seem like* will become a beautiful sunset that you'll look forward to. So when you think that it *seems like* it's over, it *seems like* you're not going to make it, it *seems like* God won't hear your prayer, it *seems like* you're lost, it *seems like* you're done, or it *seems like* it's not going to get any better, then you end up removing the power of God from the equation and thus *handcuffing* your faith. Don't *duct-tape* your belief in God to what you can see with your eyes or hear with your ears, for you must learn to truly trust in God. God is not a man that He should lie, and though He may slay me, yet will I trust Him. When you do that, then the raven will start bringing you bread and meat, your barrels will never run dry, and what the enemy stole, he'll have to pay back sevenfold. The lions that would tear your flesh will sleep at your feet, and the power of God will emanate from both your smile and your situation. I'm telling you what I know and not just something I read.

So tell Seem Like to take a hike, for there still is a God in Zion who sits high and looks low. God is not dead and never has been; neither is He blind to your situation or deaf to your call. Kick *Seem Like* out and let God in. But you have to start following God, not expecting Him to follow you. In conclusion, I say to you that you must not look to the left or to the right. Keep your eyes focused on God and His Word, and then you will become a pallbearer who will escort Seem Like to its funeral.

The End

The Blinds

(Based on a True Story)

As a small boy living in Toccoa, Georgia, I often watched a young boy named Victor lead his blind grandfather up the steep hill going into town. The grandfather carried his cane in his right hand and had his left hand on top of Victor's right shoulder. They walked along the right side of the road during all the seasons of the year. Victor Putman, being two or three years older than me, had a great responsibility; he had to be the eyes of his grandfather, and I would notice the two of them from the time I was five years old. Bear in mind that I am a baby boomer, having been born in the early fifties—before there were seat belts. I remember standing up on the floorboard of my folks' 1956 Chevrolet Bel Air in order to look out the window while holding on to the upholstered rope running across the back of the front seat. As I got older, I marveled at how the old man trusted the child to lead him wherever he needed to go. Sometimes his granddaughter Juanita Harper would lead him, and although he had several children and grandchildren, he seemed to trust Victor the most.

As the years went by and we got older, I came to know Victor better. We even went to college together at Albany State College in Albany, Georgia. Victor died at a young age, but I often think of him and his grandfather from time to time. Whenever I do think of them, I also reflect on my blind neighbor, Mr. Hosey Outlaw, who lived across the street from me. I only saw him sitting on his front porch during the spring, summer, and fall. In the summertime, my grandmother, who used to be the medicine woman of my town, had a niece we called Cousin Bessie She was heavyset and blind. She lived in Buford, Georgia, but would come up to Toccoa during the summer. My brother, my two cousins (Emory and Gary Thornton), and I used to make fun of how large her underwear was whenever my aunt would hang clothes on the clothesline. We would get into trouble whenever we tried to make them into a swing; we would bring down the clothesline every time. Heck, there was no Six Flags during those days, and the thought of swinging in a pair of drawers seemed intriguing and exciting.

I've worn glasses since the age of seven, and I was so nearsighted that my lens were almost as thick as Coke bottles, so sight has always a been precious thing to me, and the subject of sight is something that not only held my curiosity but also my interest as well. My vision was so bad that I used to wear my glasses to bed just so I could see in my dreams. But just what is sight, and what does it mean to see? Over the years, I pondered such a thought, and then I ran into Johnny, a fellow serviceman who was connected to the Vietnam War and suffered from chronic and severe PTSD. Due to the fear and paranoia caused by the condition, Johnny constantly lived behind closed blinds. Being hypervigilant, he hid from the emotional pain and nightmares caused by his involvement and participation in the Vietnam War. The blinds protected him from the sights outside that would trigger memories of many things he chose to forget; however, the blinds were impotent to prevent the resurfacing of distilled terrors that fueled his reoccurring nightmares. The blinds had a twofold purpose; they not only prevented Johnny from seeing out but also kept others from seeing in.

For some reason, I could not get Johnny, Victor and his grandfather, Cousin Bessie, and Mr. Hosey out of my mind. The Lord kept speaking to me about sight and blindness and about people and situations. My brain felt like a punch bowl holding ambrosia made of thoughts, and I could not tie it all together until He gave me this soufflé of a story.

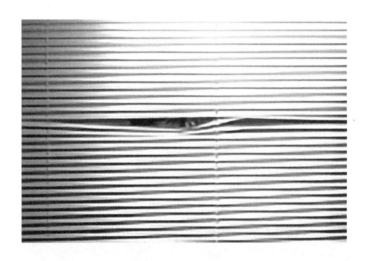

It was in the land of Wondering within the city limits of Questions where there lived Thought. Thought was very fast and speedy, as all thoughts are, for even the speed of light cannot surpass the speed of thought; light still has to travel a distance, while a thought is instantly instantaneous. Because of his speed, he could seemingly be in an unlimited number of places simultaneously. He could either be running around the walls inside your brain, or he could be jumping on the emotions of my heart. He could be on the earth, the moon, or even Mars. Thought became bored one day, having always lived in the town of Questions, and he wanted to see more of the world of ideas. Thought heard that there was an oracle by the name of Mr. Consider who facilitated the growth and development of thoughts by taking them from a single word and then developing them into concepts. Thought decided that it was time high time for him to grow up and advance; therefore, he set out on a quest to find Mr. Consider. One day, while traveling from mind to mind, he heard someone read an advertisement that stated that Mr. Consider would be hosting a sight seminar at a blind convention in the land of Discovery. Thought set out to attend that seminar. When he arrived at the convention, he found all kinds of entities and creatures present; they wanted to learn the meaning of sight and to understand what being blind really means. Present were figureheads like Mr. Mole, the Four Blind Mice, Ms. Bat, and a host of others whose names are too numerous and unimportant to mention at this point.

Mr. Consider called the convention to order. He elaborated on the qualifying experiences that backed his credentials. He made them all aware that he came into being from the mind of God when the Creator considered creating the universe, the earth, mankind, life, and all the entities throughout the endless universes of space and time. He said that he was going to employ a new strategy for the discovery of the understanding of sight and blindness. The strategy entailed breaking the assembly up into three groups for discussions. After a specified period of time, the groups would reconvene to put the answers to the questions together like pieces of a simple jigsaw puzzle. And with that said, each broke off into their respective group. One group had to deal with physical blindness. Another group discussed psychological blindness, and the third talked about spiritual blindness. Thought planned to be in all three groups simultaneously so he wouldn't miss out on anything.

The first group dealt with physical blindness, which was truly elementary, for after you got past the optic nerve and how it communicates with the centers of the brain, there really isn't a whole lot left to discover. Attendees spoke about their heightened senses of hearing, touch, and smell; they compensated for their lack of sight. But there is one thing they found to be most amazing, which is coming to comprehend and understand that the purpose of sight is to open, reveal, and enhance the world around them. Light dispels darkness, but when things are not present to process the light, then darkness prevails. Without the physical hardware to process light externally and internally, one cannot *see* what's in a room, the world, or the universe.

The second group focused on psychological blinders that are caused by self-erected obstructions and result in the inability to see reality clearly. This group determined that emotions play a key role in preventing one from seeing reality clearly. Most of the time, it is because of some traumatic experience that got buried deep down in the subconscious and got covered by current experiences, forming a coating of denial that prevents further hurt and pain. These experiences include the pain from the loss of a loved, divorce, death, or a mere breakup. The pain could've resulted from the trauma of rape or molestation or perhaps rejection and even addiction. Whatever the cause of the trauma, the end results are usually the same—the person becomes blind to the initial cause of the pain and impotent to prevent or put a stop to its devastating results. The person ends up erecting and living behind camouflaged psychological blinds in order to function and feel safe. They learn to become comfortable with their blindness, and it becomes their norm.

The third group zeroed in on spiritual blindness and concluded that evil prevents us from seeing when it erects blinds that prevent the light of the Word of God from shining through. Satanic and demonic forces position themselves in the blind spots of the mirrors of our lives so that they avoid our detection and can rob us of sight, revelation, and spiritual elevation. They are like duck hunters or deer hunters behind camouflaged screens, taking potshots at the blessing that God has sent our way. They cause us to *respond the wrong way* to the tests of life. If we don't respond the right way, the blessings get held up and even denied in some cases. For instance, if we repay good with evil, the blessing is denied. If we repay evil with evil, the blessing is put on hold until we learn better. But if we turn the other cheek and repay hate with love while giving thanks for all things, then the blinds open up, the light comes through, the enemy scatters with the darkness, Heaven opens up, and the blessings rain down.

Now it was time for them to reconvene, and when all were assembled, Mr. Consider started by saying, "Sight is more than simply a sense. It is a gift from God. Many, if not all of you, think of blindness as a condition, but I implore you to both reconsider and redefine blindness. Blindness is not only a condition, for blindness can also be a state of being. If you look at it that way, then you will understand how sometimes those without eyes can see while those with eyes cannot. Sight is not limited to the physical realm because it encompasses more than that. It includes the psychological and spiritual aspects of life as well. God created sight to allow His creatures to recognize the beauty, understanding, and glory of His creation. Sight helps us understand why we need light instead of darkness, love instead of hate, joy instead of sorrow, and happiness instead of grief. There are many creatures who have eyes but still cannot see, and there are those who do not have eyes but can."

That idea and realization shot through Thought. If he gained nothing more than that insight, then attending the convention would still have been well worth his time and all the sacrifices he'd made to be there.

We are blind to many things, and we erect blinds due to many things as well. There are some things that are hidden that we cannot see and others that are very visible that we choose not to see, like the truth concerning the reality of God and Christ. Many times, the truth has been hidden from us by conspiracies that convince us with lies. Likewise, many of us are like Johnny, hiding behind the erected blinds of our lives in sorted ways. We hide behind the blinds of our past, behind the blinds of our inadequacies and shortcomings, and behind the blinds of our addictions, as well as behind the blinds of the lies we tell ourselves and others. We also hide behind the blinds of unrealistic expectations and the blinds of prejudice, racism, and denial.

Some blinds prevent us from seeing out, while others prevent those on the outside from seeing in. Oftentimes, others have to look through our blinds and see in us the things that we cannot see in ourselves. Jesus saw something in Mary Magdalene and in the apostle Paul. God saw something in King David and in Moses. The good thing is that God sees something in you that you cannot see in yourself. You might not see out because of the blinds, but God can always see in.

You see, we are but blind sojourners in this life who are making our way up mountains called situations and through valleys called circumstances. No matter how much we think we can see, we are like Victor's grandfather in that we are blind and in need of someone that we can trust and depend on to guide us safely along our way as we travel the road toward our purpose and destiny. We need someone to keep us out of life ditches—the things that limit our ability to enjoy life fully. We need someone to keep us away from the traffic of difficulties that could ruin or even kill us. Christ is that someone. But before He can lead us, we have to become like blind Bartimaeus in Mark 10:46–53 (KJV) and discard our robes of pride, ego, self, dignity, community standing, social status, political views, and aspirations. We must be *empty* when we go to Christ in order to receive our sight. We must allow Him to become the Victor in our lives and let Him lead us up the mountains and through the valleys so that we can go back home to the kingdom of God, where we belong. I leave you with this simple prayer: "*Lord, reveal unto me the things that are hidden from the eyes of man.*" Psalm 139:23–24 says, "Search me, O God, and know my heart: try me, and know my thoughts: And see if there be any wicked way in me, and lead me in the way everlasting." Do this, Lord, because once I was blind, but through your Word and this story, now I see. Amen!

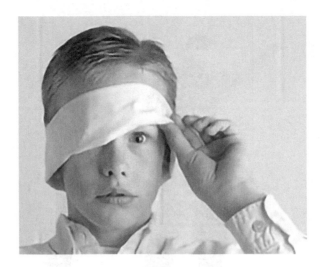

The End

Note 1: During the biblical times, a person's robe indicated his status, his authority, his position in the community, his standing, and his dignity. When Jesus called for Bartimaeus, he cast away his robe and went to Jesus; he was empty. He came before Christ empty of pride, dignity, standing, and status; he stood before him with great humility to obtain mercy.

Note 2: The Four Blind Mice symbolize the four types of spiritual sight a person can have:

1.) Foresight—seeing over the hill and down the road
2.) Insight—seeing below the surface and beyond the apparent
3.) Hindsight—seeing after the fact
4.) No Sight—you're completely blind to the fact and simply don't see at all

The Plant

Twyla was an odd individual while being the personification of normal. She was a thirty-six-year-old only child, unmarried, and the daughter of a devout evangelist. She grew up with traditional church, family, and country values. Hard work was always the pinnacle of her treasury of values and ethics. Her father, who died when she was a teenager, never collected a dime for preaching and spreading the word of God, leaving her mother to support Twyla as well as herself. She was a latchkey kid who got good grades and was always cognizant of their struggle and doing her part to bring honor to the heads of her parents. She was an unofficial social worker, philanthropist, and part-time volunteer who worked at GA Tech as a program director in charge of a program that provided computer services to quadriplegics to enhance their independence. The program focused on a voice-recognition software that allowed "quads" to communicate and live up to their fullest potentials, as it had done for Stephen Hawking. She had a burden for the homeless, the helpless, and the hopeless. Maybe it was because of her father's teachings or her mother's long suffering (she battled breast cancer for three years before dying nine years ago)? Who knows? She often wondered about it, but it didn't really matter anyway. What was important was she had identified her purpose and lived her life to fulfill it. She had received several grants to develop a more sophisticated brain-machine interface (BMI) that would control prosthetic limbs, thus providing a more natural gait and movement to amputees, especially veterans coming back from Afghanistan and Iraq. She devoted a lot of her time to proving a new theory surrounding the plasticity of the brain that believed that the brain could and would adapt to a smart prosthetic device, operating and controlling it as if it was a pair of skis, a skateboard, or a surfboard. But traditional interfaces could not properly process the neuron signals that would enable that function. She could only imagine the ramifications of her worthy goal to improve the lives of those who had suffered such loss, especially the ones who had given so much for our country's freedom, democracy, and way of life.

She had a very busy life and dated rarely. It was hard for her find a companion who would not interfere with her focus, goals, and aspirations. Because of her schedule, she could not take care of a pet, but she wanted something else living in her apartment; therefore, she elected to get a plant. Her mother loved hibiscuses, so she bought one in memory of her, and it seemed to add life to the barren surroundings. Maybe it was her motherly instincts finally beginning to surface and kick in, compelling her desire to take care of something other than herself; only God knew for sure, and He wasn't talking. Nevertheless, this was her best option in the absence of the spouse and/or children that she one day hoped to have. Her schedule was arduous, to say the least. She was getting only four to five hours of sleep each night. She woke up at 5:00 a.m. and was out of the house by 6:00 a.m., using her bike to pedal to her work and arriving by seven o'clock. On many days, lunch was out of the question as it was a luxury that her time could not usually afford, but her stamina and determination helped her reach the finish line of each day. Saying that she was driven would be an understatement. She usually arrived back home between 8:30 to 9:00 p.m. She would then shower before eating supper, which would be followed by her BMI research. If she made it to bed before 1:00 a.m., it would be as miraculous as the parting of the Red Sea. After about a week, she noticed that her plant was beginning to lose foliage and figured that it needed more sunlight, so she moved it from the living room to the patio. She bought a moisture detector and inserted it into the soil so she could determine if it was getting enough water after noticing that it had drooped as if it was withering. She went on the Internet and ordered bat guano. She thought that the special fertilizer would produce a healthy change, but she was wrong. The impotence she felt as she watched her mother die returned, and she was saddened by her plant's suffering. It needed something, but she did not know what that was. She decided to mix new soil in case the proportions weren't right and transplanted it into a new, bigger, and more colorful pot. But there was no change, and the plant's condition seemed to worsen.

As everyone knows, being on the go all the time and getting little sleep is a recipe for disaster as it weakens the immune system, and Twyla was no exception. Within a week after obtaining her plant, she came down with a strange virus that required her to be hospitalized. She was at work with the sniffles and a bit of a fever when a coworker observed her having difficulty, and then her coughing started to get outrageous. After a brief conversation with her cohort, she decided to take a sick day and go home. She gathered her belongings and was headed out the door when she abruptly fainted. Of course, 911 was called, and by the time she regained consciousness, she was in a hospital gown and lying on a bed at Emory University Hospital. She was the only child of parents who were only children themselves, so no immediate family was around for her to call on. Perhaps this was a blessing in disguise, for it gave her time to sort out so many issues in her life and recall the many things her father would talk to her about growing up. She was glad she didn't have a dog or cat but sad that she didn't have a husband and children or family. She was a bit groggy, either because of the medication or the lack of rest. When she was awake and lucid, she would pray, watch TV (something she usually never had time for), and try to make the best of a bad situation. She overheard one of the nurses talking about the possibility of Legionnaires' disease being connected to her condition and prayed to God that it wasn't the case. Her doctor came to her a few hours later and explained that she had contracted walking pneumonia. She would not be going home soon. Her only comfort at the time was her father's voice saying in her head, "God works in mysterious ways." She had forgotten, overlooked, or simply ignored too many things when it came to her upbringing—all of which seemed to cascade down her memory like the waters flowing from the top of Toccoa Falls on a rainy day.

She grew very depressed; her condition was touch and go for about a week. To exacerbate the situation, she had no visitors. She thought that her workmates or so-called friends would take the time to at least call if they didn't have the time to come by. She then thought about her plant and grew concerned about its condition. As her health continued to decline, it became imperative for her to find some way to have it with her as it had become a surrogate family member for her. They changed her type of medication, her dosage, and even her room but to no avail. After a couple of days, she became encouraged as they moved her into a regular private room, but she was not out of the woods by a long shot. She contacted one of her office mates, asking her to go to her apartment to get her plant and bring it to her room. The associate and the property-management manager were obliged to honor her request. When the plant arrived the following day, she found that it had withered more, and being without leaves, it looked as though it was almost dead. She too had almost given up hope and had resigned herself to death. One day, she awoke from a nap to the sound of the voice of a young high school volunteer named Sonny. Sonny was talking to the plant and giving it water while using a medicine dropper. Sonny noticed the plant seemed to respond and swore he could hear it talk. Twyla pretended to be asleep. She discovered his schedule for daily volunteering, and every day for a week, she pretended to nap whenever he would enter the room in order to listen to him talk to her plant. Within three days, she noticed that the plant was no longer drooping and had started to put on new foliage. After the seventh day, she pretended to wake up while he was there. He introduced himself, and they had a long, wonderful conversation; the young man seemed to be wise beyond his years. From then on, she looked forward to his visits, and the staff began to see a remarkable improvement in her condition. After a week, she and her plant were discharged during the middle of the day, but she begged to stay until late evening, hoping to see and talk with Sonny one last time. She convinced herself that the reason for her delay was her desire to discover his secret for taking care of her plant, but it was much deeper than that. Sonny had caused her to reconsider her priorities in life, for if she ever had a child, she would want him or her to be as smart, as caring, and as compassionate as him. He seemed to know just what to say, how to say it, and when to say it. Sonny had the zeitgeist of the seventies and eighties—when people had an imagination that was capable of allowing them to put themselves in other people's shoes. While waiting for him to arrive, she went on the Internet and downloaded an e-book of short stories that was entitled *Teachable Moments*, and she read a short story called "Hiding Out." The story caused her to evaluate her motives for being driven. Perhaps it wasn't really to help amputees but rather to escape her evaluating her life and motives.

When Sonny arrived, they talked for an hour or two. When she asked him what he did to save her plant, he simply said that he talked to it, for the hibiscus was lonely. He said that he sensed the plant's need to have a relationship with someone, and he therefore became that someone. He explained that the new pot, the fertilizer, the water, and the sunshine were necessary, but they weren't what the plant needed or wanted most. He said she gave it what it needed physically but neglected to discover what it wanted emotionally and perhaps even spiritually. The plant had sensed her despair and felt her need to keep busy to avoid thinking about what the most important things in life are—things like family, peace, love, compassion, and connection with Almighty God. He went on to say that she and the plant had a lot in common, for she desired a relationship filled with concern and care. That's why he took the time to make himself available, showing her compassion while allowing her access to his thoughts and feelings. Suddenly, she realized that those were the things that had caused her recovery. She wanted to give him the plant to show her gratitude and appreciation, but he refused. He explained that the plant wanted a relationship with her personally, not a relationship with her through him. He informed her that the same is true when it comes to Almighty God; He wants a personal relationship with us all, not one through our pastors, our priests, our friends, or our mothers and/or fathers. God had a reason for creating us to become a part of His family. The Bible says, "But as many as received him, to them gave he power to become the sons of God, even to them that believe on his name" (John 1:12). He then rolled her wheelchair to the nurse's station and suddenly vanished. None of the nurses or employees working there had ever seen or heard of him. Maybe there's a lot more to be said about Hebrews 13:2, which says, "Be not forgetful to entertain strangers: for thereby some have entertained angels unawares." Maybe we need to also entertain the idea that the whole Bible can be summed up in this sentence: *God wants to have a personal relationship with you and me!* Twyla finally got it, and I hope and pray that you do too.

The End

The Sword

The happenings in Alex's life had troubled him for quite some time, but now the problem had turned into a genuine crisis. He wondered if he was cursed after experiencing thirty years of unfortunate, uncanny, obscure circumstances that seemed to defy any explanation. He had come to the end of his rope. All he knew was something had to give, and he didn't want it to be him; however, it was what it was. Running away, quitting, and taking his own life seemed to be his only viable choices, and he reluctantly considered all of them. Needless to say, high on the list of Christian taboos and societal no-no's is suicide. *But what the heck?* he thought. He surmised that God wasn't listening to his prayers anyway, and perhaps He wasn't looking as well. Even though he was a baptized believer, the core of his beliefs was in jeopardy because adverse conditions and abnormal negative occurrences were causing him to question the reality of God.

He thought of his friend Charles Smith—a retired pharmacist who lived in Toccoa, Georgia—and decided to pay him a visit. Charles's insight had always been helpful to him in the past; his nonjudgmental insight and elderly wisdom saved his butt plenty of times and prevented him from making costly mistakes by challenging his (Alex's) reasoning and causing him to evaluate his own faith. He traveled to the mountains of northeastern Georgia to sit a while with his friend, stopping along the way to go to the top of Currahee Mountain. As a teenager, he often went to the top of the mountain to pray and seek God's face. It seemed that he was long overdue for a visit with God on that mountain. "Lord," he prayed, "my soul is weary, and I need to somehow make sense of all of this. Forgive me if I falter, but I need a breakthrough and divine intervention to keep me from giving up." After saying that, he went to the sleepy town where he could find his Caucasian friend, who was almost thirty years older than him.

After sharing his thoughts, emotions, and pain with Charles, Charles told him the story of a young man who had similar experiences. His friend began the story.

To say that Itsume was born under a bad sign would be somewhat sacrilegious and an understatement although he thought it more times than it rained in the state of Washington. Nothing he did came easy as he was always warring to complete the simplest of tasks—no matter how honorable, how righteous, how worthy, or how worthwhile. He thought the epitome of it all was his becoming a soldier in a war he did not believe in or approve of. He believed that sacrificing himself for the welfare of his family and loved amounted to the greater good and therefore made it justifiable.

Unemployment in the black community was at an all-time high (40 percent) and had become a real problem in America. He got married. While he was in college and had been married for a year, he enlisted in the Air Force to support his wife. He thought that after four years, he would return to GA Tech under the GI Bill and get a job so he could send his wife back to Spelman College. Both realized the importance of completing a college education. Being black, being a free thinker, and being a genius were all concentric circles of a bull's-eye that hung on his life, and Jim Crow racists and white-supremacist guardians used it for target practice. But there was something going on here that was greater than mere racism—something higher than evil spells, black-cat bones, and voodoo curses—all of which he considered in an effort to understand and explain his uncanny struggles.

He found himself on the other side of the world—in a small third world village outside Manila, frying in the morning heat of the Philippines. He sat across from the marketplace and next to an old Filipino man and had tears streaming down his cheeks. Under normal circumstances, suicide would never have been an option, nor did it figure into the equation that would make sense of the reality he longed to be free of, but something had to explain the madness that forever surrounded him. He just couldn't seem to find answers. As so many people do when they can no longer bear unquenchable pain, he cried out until his pain robbed his vocal cords of any sound. Weeping and death were all that seemed to be left, and death had taken a hiatus. For some reason, he felt compelled to share his thoughts and feelings with the old man, unafraid of his personal business being broadcasted. Itsume began talking about the emotional pain he endured as a child when his dad didn't think he was his father and punished him severely yet differently from his brother who was older than him by nineteen months. It hurt Itsume so much that he attempted suicide at age 9 at their neighborhood's recreation-center swimming pool. He shared how he started working when he was seven years old because his dad would not buy him toys like he did for his brother. He became independent at an early age, buying his own toys, school clothes, and even life insurance by shining shoes, raking leaves, washing dishes, and cutting grass. He recalled the integration of his public school in 1965 and how he was treated like a leper for being the only minority in all his classes when he was only fourteen years old. He still bore the emotional scars of that experience; no one would sit by him or talk to him, and his teachers ignored him whenever he raised his hand to participate in class. He recalled how his first cousin intentionally stabbed him in the throat with a butcher's knife when he was only sixteen; another eighth of an inch and he would've severed his windpipe. He wept as he remembered how his father wouldn't teach him how to drive like he did for his brother, causing him to fail his driver's test—the first test he ever failed in his life; he, therefore, had to teach himself.

Suddenly, the old man turned to him and spoke to him in English, much to his surprise. "So it is in the life of a man whom God chooses to use. The Blacksmith of the Universe will place you on the anvil of life, take the hammer of circumstance into His hand, and hit you with it until He has you in the shape He wants you to be in. He will then take you off the anvil and stick you into burning-hot coals made of trials and disappointments for a period of time that is known only by him. After removing you from the coals, he will place you back on that anvil only to hammer, knock, and beat you some more until He determines if you've learned what He's trying to teach you or if your response is consistent with His Word and the teachings of Christ. And after you have been tried by the fire, He will dip you in cold, clean water to forge you with relief—no matter how temporary that might be. After bringing you up from the water, He will look at you and feel assured that, like a well-forged sword, you won't break on Him in battle or lose your edge while engaging the enemy. The enemy has broken and destroyed many men who went out on their own and did not allow Yahweh to take them through this process during their lives."

By divine revelation, Itsume's eyes were opened, and his understanding was awakened. Suddenly, everything made sense, and he finally understood what God had been up to and doing in his life. Itsume's remorse and sadness changed into joy and peace; he was humbled not only by the fact that God chose to take him through this but also by the fact that He was there with him the whole time. What a wonderful thing to realize! God had performed His Word in his life, and he realized the truth in the Scriptures. They say "To him that much is given much is required," "All things work together for good for them that Love the Lord and are called according to His purpose," and "Though He may slay me yet will I trust Him." It became clear to him that although he might not see it or understand it, God will always show up in his life and circumstance if he trusts Him and waits on Him. When He shows up, He also shows out, for He forever exceeds whatever we might ask for! At last, every situation, every circumstance, every heartache, every problem, and every pain suddenly had meaning, and he found comfort in the knowledge that he could not have survived them all without God's presence orchestrating the events for his (Itsume's) greater good. He (God the Father) had indeed performed His Word in Itsume's life, and now all he had to do was to buckle up his seat belt of trust and hang on for the ride.

I hope this opens the eyes of your understanding and gives you comfort, for God is not a man—a being that may lie. So go forth, Grasshopper, and be the sword God has created you to be and remember that His eye is on the sparrow and is on you too.

The story Charles shared shook Alex like it did Itsume, and from then on, Alex never questioned God again but simply buckled up his seat belt with excitement and the determination to serve Him and follow Him and the willingness to be transformed into the image of Christ. What about you?

The End

The Missing Ingredient

By Larry "Skeeter" Mance

A young mother wanted to learn how to make homemade biscuits. She had always enjoyed her mother's biscuits. She was a mother herself now with a precocious 3 year old (much like herself when she was a child). She had not spoken with her mother for 7 years due to some argument or misunderstanding that never should have occurred in the first place. Nonetheless, the young mother used 2 cups of plain flour along with the milk, salt, and shortening required by the recipe she recalled from watching her mother as a child. But every time she tried to make the biscuits they would be flat rather than fluffy like her mom's. She changed the proportions in the recipe hoping that would solve the problem but it never did. Finally, she just gave up and quit trying.

Two years later, she got a call from the small town hospital some 30 miles away where she grew up telling her that her mother was deathly ill and that she should come as soon as possible for her mother had been asking for her being lucid for short periods between falling in and out of consciousness. Her daughter was now 5 years old and she thought it was vital that she see her grandmother at least once; but more importantly, she had come to realize how much she really loved her mother and now, being a mother herself, she would not want her daughter to treat her like she had treated her mother. So, it was imperative that she get there while there was still time and she prayed while her daughter played on the greyhound bus that ferried them to the next town over.

Arriving at the hospital, she rushed with her daughter to her mother's room where a first cousin posted up at her mother's bedside like an NBA center under the rim at a championship game. She relieved her cousin who graciously took charge of her daughter so she could be alone with her mother. As she sat after pulling up a chair from across the room, she began to recall her childhood; she remembered her mother dressing her up, bathing her and combing her hair before either taking her or sending her to Sunday School if she was too sick to do it herself. She thought of the Christmas speeches her mother rehearsed with her and her favorite Sunday school song "Yes, Jesus Loves Me". She began to recall the bedtime stories she read to her like Jonah and the Whale, Daniel in the Lion's Den, Noah and the Ark, David and Goliath, Sampson and Delilah, Moses and the Ten Commandments, Joseph and the coat of many colors, the Birth of Christ, and the Easter Story. She decided it was time to teach her daughter the bedtime prayer "Now I lay me down to sleep".

She and her mother had a wonderful fulfilling relationship up until her second year of middle school for it was then that things began to go awry. She tried to determine if it was because of her father's death in Vietnam (a God Fearing tunnel rat who loved his God, his family and his country) or if it was due to the group of so called friends she depended on to fill the void left by his death that influenced her to try drugs and alcohol insisting that God is dead, the Bible isn't real and that Creation never took place but rather evolution instead. Whatever the reason, it was then that the decay started in their relationship like a severe termite infestation in a pine forest. For you don't see them until it's too late. But she was determined not to let that happen and prayed to God that He would allow her mother to awaken long enough to tell her how sorry she was and how wrong it was for her to allow some misunderstanding to cause such demise. The shame of it all is she couldn't even recall what the argument had been about. While thinking of how "history repeats itself" she was raising a daughter alone like her mother since her husband had been the target of a sniper's bullet in Afghanistan a year ago.

"Baby...Baby" she heard her mother call realizing that she had drifted off into a deep sleep. This is how her mother used to wake her for church, for school, for everything. She remember how she told her mother to stop calling her a baby since she was grown now (or so she thought) and her mother telling her that no matter how old she became that she would always be her "Baby". Suddenly she realized what a great mother God had gifted her being a woman of virtue, of character always being her mother and not compromising to be her friend. Her mother now became a compass for her to navigate the waters of motherhood and, with God's help, she and her daughter would be just fine.

"Thank you Jesus" her mother cried "For you have brought the prodigal home and answered my prayers". She heard her mother pray out loud as she had so many times before (a pleasant memory that somehow became lost in the cracks of her mind). "You performed Your Word once again in my life by 'Never leaving me nor forsaking me' and 'never denying me any good thing'.

"Baby, Momma missed you so much and I'm sorry for the fight we had. I tried to call you so many times and reconcile with you but you changed your number and I never knew your address. But time is short and we need to forgive one another while we're both on this side of the grave".

"I know Momma. I'm sorry for how I've treated you and I was wrong in allowing something so trivial to come between the love we have for one another. I was young and foolish thinking that I knew everything and it's only now that I begin to even discover the questions".

From that point on it seemed as if time stood still and the indescribable sweet aroma of peace and joy that permeates from long awaited forgiveness replaced the sterile hospital smell of that room. Eventually, the young mother brought her daughter in to meet her grandmother and the three of them were fulfilled in ways words could never describe. Finally, the young mother thought to ask her mother for her biscuit recipe. She explained that she had tried so many times to make biscuits for her 5 year old but they would never rise.

"Are you using plain or self-rising flour?" her mother asked. She answered plain. "Well that's the problem…you have to add baking powder if you're using plain but in self rising flour the baking powder has already been added to the flour. She realized that without that ingredient her desired outcome would never be realized. Her mother said, "There's something I want you to learn about all this. We live our lives like making biscuits. We want them to be light, fluffy, tasty and sightly to the eyes, fragrant to the nose and sweet to the palate. And no mater how we change the proportions, if we don't have the right ingredients it will never turn out right. Jesus is the ingredient we need in our lives to make us rise above the situation, above the circumstance, above the heartache and the pain. We can change our homes, change our mates, change our jobs, but if He is not in the equation or the formula for our process of living then life will always be flat and unsavory".

In less than an hour her mother passed away and was gone but her final words would rest with the young mother for the rest of her time here on this physical plane; not only that, but she too would tell and remind her own baby for the rest of her life and if God saw fit, she would do the same with every grand child, great grand child and so forth from generation to generation. So while you're making biscuits (whether those biscuits be getting ready for work or vacation, going to school or to church, no matter where, no matter when or no matter what), don't leave out the main ingredient and include the Lord in all your ways, all your dreams and in all your getting.

The End

Applying the Brakes

(Based on a True Story Told by Uncle Ned)

This old straight-shift Ford truck of a story is getting ready to take off the road, and if you got the time or the mind to, then hop in, and we'll talk a spell. Close you' door now, and don't worry about seat belts 'cause they didn't make 'em back then. No, sir, I don't mind if you smoke—long as the window's cracked—just as long as you listen. All I ask is, for God's sake, please don't cut the cheese as it might cause me to forget and lose my focus. I'm prone to do so from time to time. Heck, if you're as bad as my wife, it might even cause me to wreck, which I did the winter befoe' last—when it was nineteen degrees and she released one of her SBDs, which stands for "silent but deadly." I was taking her to Walmart for groceries and a manicure. Man, I'd never seen anything like it. It not only singed the hairs in my nostrils but also fogged up these dang windows, and I ran off the road. Well, me being eighty-three years old with Parkinson's and a lead foot didn't help none either, but I still say that it was the fog from the cheese that was the culprit. Naw, nothing too bad—just clipped a couple of mailboxes, but they charged me wid a ten-thousand-dollar fine and destruction of government property since the mailboxes were out in front of the post office. Now just calm down, young feller. I was just joshin' ya! Now you know why I took the inside door handle off on your side, and the window won't let all the way down. Gotcha' again! I like to see the expressions on people's faces when I tell 'em that. Truth is, my grandson's fiancée' broke that handle off when I told 'em that story while giving them a ride home after their car broke down at the picture show last week. But the fog and the cheese part are true. The moral of that story is don't drive yo' wife nowhere the next day when you done had pinto beans for supper the night befoe'!

You see, I knew this feller once they called Trim Master. Said a guy named Michael Delaughter gave him that name. But befoe' I could ask him why Mike chose that name, he told me this about himself as he sat on the porch close to dark wid his dog at his feet, thinking back over his life, pondering the many wonderful things God had done to save and sustain him over the years. Yeah, I know. First gear's a little rough, and the clutch is acting up, but here goes. I'm not gonna tell you everything—just a few things to perk your interest and hopefully make my point. It was important for him to take inventory of the provisions of God by remembering how God had performed His Word in his life lest he become unappreciative like the children of Israel in the wilderness as they journeyed from Egypt to the Promised Land. The more God did for them, the more they forgot, and the more they forgot, the more they whined and complained in their ungratefulness. He agreed with an inner voice that said, "It's dangerous to take God for granted." How well did he know that, for in 2001, he lost his right lung due to Agent Orange exposure from his time in the Vietnam War. His sister Pearlena said they lost him three times on the operating table, and if that wasn't enough, five years later, three blood clots occurred simultaneously in his right leg—between the base of his knee and his groin. It resulted in his having no blood pressure on the entire right side of his body. Had it not been for two outside doctors—one from China and one from Jamaica—he would have lost that leg, and now he only has about 40 percent feeling in it due to the surgery and the deep-vein thrombosis still residing somewhere in his upper right thigh. But he wasn't complaining. He was happy in knowing that God was with him and the attacks that the enemy perpetrated to end his life in order to prevent him from fulfilling his purpose had been for naught. Oftentimes, God will allow tragically startling, catastrophic events to enter our lives in order to show us that He is still with us and that His promises to us have been vouchsafed and sealed.

It started with the jigsaw puzzle of the places he had lived and worked inside and outside the United States, but his recollections did not end there, for the mental journey he had begun zip-lined him into a past that often was just too painful to remember. Like a huge ship capsizing in the sea of his mind, he recalled highlights of his Mobile, Alabama, experience, examining the wreckage of a failed marriage that happened mostly due to the rejection of his in-laws residing there. Only Uncle Kitrell and Aunt Jessie made him feel welcome and not less-than. As his oldest daughter, Tameesha, would often say to him years later, "It is what it is," and make no mistake about it. Trim and his wife had been having marital problems after the birth of his son, their second child, and she left him, going back to live with her parents in Mobile. He previously was unemployed, but as soon as she left, he got a job at the Environmental Protection Agency with the help of Cornell Seymour, a longtime friend, and Barbara Boone. Although he loved and missed her very much, he was getting used to being without his wife. After a couple of months, I believe, she came to Atlanta and spent the weekend with him, seducing him to come to Mobile for the sake of their family. This was truly a paramount and executive decision to be made, and he was very torn. He was more torn than lettuce in a garbage disposal, more torn than a piñata on Cinco de Mayo, and more torn than the loser of a pit-bull fight. *Shredded* would be a better word because he had to decide between sticking with a good-paying job with benefits and having no job at all, between being selfish and not being selfish by keeping his family together regardless of the sacrifice, and between keeping his marital vows—made before Almighty God—and rationalizing why he should stay in Atlanta. But his conscience needled him because when his son was born, he had jaundice so bad that the child wasn't expected to live. He recalled how he slept on the tile floor in the hallway, below the hospital's nursery window, pleading with God to spare his son's life and promising Him that if He did, he would give his son back to the Creator. God heard his plea, and the next day, both child and mother were discharged as if nothing had ever been wrong. Remembering his promise and the desire to honor it and not wanting to have future regrets concerning the raising of his children, he reluctantly elected to quit the job and go to

Mobile, praying and hoping to find a job once he got there. His fear of what would happen to his son if he did not keep his vow was greater than his fear of not finding a job once he pulled up stakes. It was wintertime, and although temperatures were warmer than in Atlanta, it was still cold, especially at night. When he got there, he was not welcomed by her to stay at their house, so he slept in the back seat of his car in a Piggly Wiggly parking lot for a couple of weeks. But his wife made sure he had plenty of blankets and quilts to keep warm. Weeks later, he secured a position with Ingalls Shipbuilders in Pascagoula, Mississippi. He would work in submarine overhaul as a rate setter.

Months later, his wife got the sad news that her father's cancer had returned. It originated in his prostate and now had spread to his colon and his lungs and brain. All his father-in-law wanted was to see his first and only grandson, Aurious Daa, walk before he died, and God, in His mercy, allowed that. As a matter of fact, he died shortly after Trim's son took his first steps. This was devastating to Trim's wife, and things got so bad she could barely function. It became both apparent and imperative that he quit his job in order to help her with their two-year-old and six-month-old. Sacrificing himself for the sake of those he loved had become something he was accustomed to, for it was his reason for enlisting in the military during the Vietnam War. The military experience was even worse than civilian life, for the Air Force owned him right down to his very body, and there was nothing anyone could do about the racism and injustices blacks suffered while in the hands of Uncle Sam. Just to give you an example, there was a time when he was ordered to take an experimental drug they called space tabs, and to this day, he's unaware of its purpose or aftereffects. Many were wrongly given dishonorable discharges—not to mention the ones who lost their lives from so-called friendly fire. The black soldiers returning from the war not only were spat on and ostracized by the general public here at home, but they were also denied services in public places like restaurants, denied access to housing, not allowed the use of the restroom, and still could not gain entry into country clubs. But the worst battle was him having to fight the Veterans Administration to get the benefits and compensation he earned from being damaged by the war. He often wondered if his soul would ever experience peace while it was in this world, for it appeared that he had to fight everyone for everything—right down to the right to exist.

But that's not what this story is about, so forgive me. I shall recover my focus. It's about Trim Master's experiences that demonstrated the vouchsafed and sealed promises of God in his life. So where was I? Oh yeah. After resigning, Trim tried to buy and run a small run-down convenience store in the Hillsdale area, but it was more than he could handle and manage. I failed to mention that while in service, he had been in a bad car accident while on duty and on base that resulted in him being hospitalized for months. The trauma from the accident took its toll even more whenever it revisited him both physically and emotionally. Needless to say, his wife was in no shape to render assistance. He met a guy in the Hillsdale area who was named Big Earl Hill, and he became his best friend and running dog. Earl was around six feet three and weighed between 200 and 220 pounds. Earl was a longshoreman and a member of Local Union No. 1410 on the docks there in Mobile. Bear in mind that this was before containerized shipment took over, costing many black longshoremen their jobs and livelihoods. Earl called Trim Lil' Daddy or LD, for Trim Master was small in stature. He's around five feet six and 120 pounds soaking wet. But he did not lack courage and perseverance. Earl talked LD into becoming a longshoreman and took him down to the docks to show him the ropes. Little Daddy joined Local 1410 and was well respected by the officers in the union, for many were uneducated and lacked the ability to successfully represent their constituents when it came to grievances. Local 1410 discovered LD to be invaluable not only because of his GA Tech roots but also because he had studied under and was mentored by Dr. Sherman Dallas, a well-known federal arbitrator during the seventies and eighties—when collective bargaining was in its heyday.

Because of his size, most crew foremen would not pick LD to work with them until Big Earl would tell them not to judge his size. They always paired LD with Big Earl, and the two of them would throw and stack hundred-pound burlap sacks of grain in the belly of a cargo ship. Sometimes they'd reach as high as fifty feet during a twelve-hour shift. The burlap would cause LD to have blisters on the tips of all ten fingers simultaneously; they'd hurt so much that his wife would have to unzip his pants in order for him to urinate. How LD got both the strength and endurance to toss those sacks can only be accounted for by his prayers being answered whenever he asked Almighty God to loan him the strength to do so. At least, that's what he told me.

During the course of all of this, LD's wife announced that she was pregnant with their third child, Alesha, and the stress factor seemed to soar. Due to a bitter argument, LD's wife left him and went to live with her mother, taking the children with her. He missed taking his three-year-old and one-year-old to a primitive Baptist church in Tomonville more than anything, for he had promised God that if the Almighty would give him healthy children, he would give them back to Him. In a few months, his baby girl was born, and he consistently tried to mend the relationship and get his wife back home, but in-law interference was far greater than he could have ever imagined. After LD's mother received a phone call that threatened his life, she begged and eventually persuaded him to leave Mobile and return to Georgia. It was the hardest thing he ever did in his entire life because doing it meant leaving his children. After unloading the U-Haul truck in Toccoa, LD set out for Atlanta to find his longtime friend Harry E. Crew, for he shared things with Crew that he never shared with anyone. Their bond could not be described with mere words, for they related to each other in so many ways. They artistically, spiritually, and metaphysically shared thoughts and ideas that most people never even have. It was Crew who taught him how to cook.

After he found Crew and shared the chain of painful events that led him there, Crew, having a one-bedroom apartment at Limetree Apartments, offered him the sanctuary of his living-room floor. He told him he could stay there until he could find a job and get back on his feet. Anyway, a few months passed by before Trim Master secured a position with APC Skills (a division of Alexander Proudfoot Company, a management consultant firm); before securing it, he had worked for a while with the Nuclear Assurance Corporation as an operative that prepared and bound reports of shipments of nuclear waste and tracked those shipments. All his money went to child support, and he did not have enough to afford his own place, so Crew's living-room floor continued to be a godsend. He paid his friend what he could afford in order to stay there. The management-consultant position involved a lot of travel and relocation, but his expense account permitted him to be on his own. He initially moved to West Bend, Wisconsin, and then he went to Kansas City, Kansas, and Dothan, Alabama. Finally, he went to the West Indies.

It was after he started working for APC that his wife filed for divorce, which was a devastating blow to Trim Master. He still loved her and his children with every fiber of his being. He witnessed to me that there wasn't a day that went by without him thinking of them constantly or a night without him dreaming of them. Existing without them was torture and seemingly futile. He prayed to be spared the experience of being in a courtroom with her while a judge issued the decree of divorce, and his prayer was answered. God had blessed him by arranging for his job to relocate him to Port of Spain, and while the divorce proceedings were occurring, he was bodysurfing at Maracas Beach with thirty Rastafarians and eating white shark and drinking fresh coconut milk.

Bodysurfing at the white sandy beach, having emerald-green, clear water with smooth flat stones (mixed with pyrite or silver nitrate) that glistened in the sun like silver and gold coins/doubloons was a daily ritual that he enjoyed with two friends—Jamie Contis and John Gedeon. Both of them were from Pittsburg. John never left the island, and who would want to leave a place where the fruit is always plentiful and sweet, where hummingbirds are like flies, and where it's always spring? Every race under the sun lived there without racial problems. I certainly wouldn't!

Port of Spain was not a tourist trap since tourism was not their number one industry. The island assembled cars, made some of the finest rum in the world, and exported natural gas and many other goods. It truly was a paradise that was only surpassed by the garden of Eden itself. Trim experienced culture shock there because for the first time in his life, he lived in a country where black people were in control. Needless to say, he quickly learned to *lime* and *fete* (Ask a Trini what those words mean, for the definitions on the Internet do not do the terms justice).

This digression was not meant to be an ad for some travel agency, so I'll get back to the story. While he described all of this to me, I became somewhat jealous, but I should've held the jealousy back for a while, for what he told me next truly won my envy. It had nothing to do with living on the side of a mountain—on the ninth floor of the Trinidad Hilton—for six months, having Columbian coffee on the balcony, nor did it have anything to do with the aromas of flowers within two feet of the hummingbirds; It had nothing to do with the five-thousand-dollar-per-week expense account. His net pay was the same as his gross because he worked outside the USA; therefore, his wages could not be taxed. It had nothing to do with the fact that he never cashed a paycheck for over a year. Rather, it was waking up on the beach to see a full rainbow in the sky after having camped there after a night of bodysurfing beneath a full moon. How many people can say that the first thing they saw when they opened their eyes in the morning was a full rainbow without the presence of rain? That's what got my envy! Many people do not know that a full rainbow signifies an omen that announces a significant change, which usually involves moving and/or relocation. It warns of a new journey, and it would do you good to remember that. So was the case with Trim Master, for after having lived and worked there for almost one and a half years, his application for the renewal of his work permit/visa was denied. The only way he could remain there was to marry. He had several possibilities that he considered for marriage, like Maggie Singh (a Punjabi East Indian), Cathy Camps (a Trini), Janet Rudder (a Trini), Amanda Esponet (a Trini), Elizabeth Butler (a Guyanese), and Glencie Watson (a Bajan).

However, he was still smoking from the fire, being recently divorced. Even though his romantic interests were numerous, real, and sincere, he did not want to marry on the rebound and thought it wise not to marry at all—no matter how tempting the beauties or the possibilities might be. His love for his small children and his immediate family outweighed whatever feelings he had for the afore-mentioned women. Each had a piece of his heart, and his feelings for each were great and intense. Some say that composer, songwriter, performer, and R & B artist Prince didn't write and record the song "International Lover" until he happened to meet Trim in an airport as he returned to the States for four days to settle his affairs here. I was just kidding about the "International Lover" thing but serious about the rest. Now let's get back to the story.

Trim was being kicked out of the country, and when he arrived at Port of Spain's Piarco Airport, he suddenly became ill and started hemorrhaging. It appeared that all the stress, packing, and lug-gage-lifting brought on a severe case of the hemorrhoids, and the blood on the seat of his pants proved that he was bleeding profusely. He knew that he had to get off his feet and attend to this medical emergency quickly, for flying at this point would either result in him sitting in a pool of blood or being hospitalized in a third-world country, where the medical facilities and care are questionable. After praying for guidance, he suddenly remembered to call Madelyn C. (a Grenadian), whom I forgot to mention. Madelyn was older, very well off, and had been Trim's friend with benefits that he met while living at the Maraval area of Trinidad. Madelyn was indeed a godsend, for she came to Trim's rescue, picking him up and taking him back to her house, where she nursed him back to health. She bathed him, cooked his food, and bought his medicine for three solid weeks. For three weeks, everybody from the company he worked for and his family and friends looked for him; it seemed as though he had disappeared off the face of the planet. After his health returned, he boarded a plane and flew back to the United States.

I could tell you about him starting electronics school at North Georgia Technical School in Clarkesville, Georgia. I could tell you about him working for Dennis Hayes at Hayes Microcomputer Products and studying robotics in Northern California. I could tell you about him obtaining his CDL (commercial driver's license) and driving 18-wheelers for Swift Transportation or how he almost lost his life at the Zulu Lounge on Prospect Avenue in Kansas City, Kansas. I could even tell you about him living for a while in Walnut Creek, California, and tasting wine in Napa Valley every Sunday or performing his poetry in jazz clubs in San Francisco and Oakland, California, but I won't because all of those and more are in his autobiography entitled *So Much Left Unsaid*. I am, however, going tell you about him keeping the promise he made to his daddy when he married at twenty years old. He promised to finish his bachelor's degree at GA Tech, and he would keep that promise by going back to Tech when he was forty-four and finishing his degree when he was forty-six. And last but not least, I will tell you the story about him and Ms. Cobb. So let's get started 'cause it's gettin' late.

Well, a lot transpired wid Trim, as you can probably guess. Jumping episodes and sagas, I'll start at when he was driving 18-wheelers for Swift Transportation Company. He was a team driver with Thomas and going from Mount Holly, North Carolina, to Trinidad, Canada, three times a week in the wintertime. It was when the tail started waggin' the dog as he went across a high bridge on his way to Canada that he decided to get off the road or die. He knew he would end up being a fatality if he didn't get off that road. With that said, he went back to Toccoa and soon reconnected with an ex-fiancée, who later became his second wife. After moving back to Atlanta (where she lived), he got a job as a computer technician with the company that had the IT contract for the CDC (Centers for Disease Control). In 1995, when the company lost the contract, he decided that it was time to go back to Tech and finish his bachelor's; his kids were grown and emancipated. He applied only to discover that Tech denied him entry. Over the years, he would take a class or two (whatever he could afford and whenever he could afford it) until he got his credit hours down to the point where he only needed thirty hours to graduate. He was shocked when his application was denied, so he called GA Tech to find out the reason. Finally speaking with the vice president of academic affairs, he was told that Dr. Lloyd Byars (the dean of the school of management) denied his reentry. Dr. Byars believed that he, Trim, had withdrawn so many times over the years that he, Dr. Byars, didn't believe he wanted a degree from Tech. Trim explained that he never flunked out of Tech and that he worked full-time and went to school full-time and that the records would show that he did not have a student loan. He told the VP that he had no choice but to withdraw whenever he ran out of money because Tech wasn't going to let him attend for free. Trim emphatically appealed Dr. Byars's decision.

A couple of weeks later, the VP informed Trim that Dr. Byars said he would allow him back in Tech but that he would apply the ten-year rule. That meant that Trim would lose any credit hours over ten years old; now he needed ninety credit hours in order to graduate. But Trim pulled that arrow out of his chest, got down on his knees, and talked with God and entered Tech on May or June of 1995. Things were rough, but he hung in there. In 1996, the Olympics came to Atlanta, and he worked as an assistant station manager; he was in in charge of supervising the transportation of Olympic officials and athletes. It was after the Olympics ended that he began to have marital problems, and these resulted in his wife putting all his belongings on the curb. But before then, his first wife went after him for back child support, and this resulted in him being handcuffed and arrested in front of his son, who had been attending Morehouse for the past year. That was the most degrading and humiliating experience he had ever endured. He contacted his mother, and she sent his second wife five thousand dollars so he could pay the court and be released and complete his bachelor's degree. He was driving a 1963 Volvo PV544 that ended up being his apartment when he lost all his possessions. He and a friend, Elizabeth Miller, gathered up a few clothes and toiletries and his Bible and headed for GA Tech. He was determined not to let anyone cause him to fail this time.

His decision was paramount and a no-brainer. Later that night, he pulled his classic Volvo into the GA Tech student center's parking lot. Trim stealthily entered the parking lot. His sister asked him a question once, which was "How do you eat an elephant?" The answer was "One bite at a time." Considering his elephant—finishing Tech while being broke, homeless, and jobless—proved too much at the moment, so he prayed and slept vertically, and in the morning, he had to start chewing. But he brushed his teeth and washed up every morning in the men's room of the student center and made all his classes. Having fasted before, he knew he would be hungriest on his third day. It would be the weekend by then, and he found himself going to a trash can outside the building so he could forage for food. Suddenly, he thought of walking over to one of the campus ministries for help. While walking down the fraternity row, he smelled the barbeque of the Catholic ministry. He walked inside, and the priest was talking with one of the students; he was holding a fat, juicy hamburger in his hand, while others went to and fro with hands full of food. Reluctantly he spoke with the priest about his situation and even explained that he was hungry and had no money. The priest told him that he would pray for him and sent him on his way. He walked there because he didn't have gasoline, and on his walk back, he had two main thoughts. The first was "How could a man with a calling from God turn a hungry person away, especially in the midst of a cookout?" And the second was "Man, I sure wouldn't mind having a Papa John's hand-tossed pizza right about now." As he walked, he remembered the words of his pastor, Rev. Calhoun Sims, who told him that when it comes to ministers, "Some were sent, and others just went." He reached the student center and sat in one of the comfortable chairs near a window on the second floor, where all the eateries were located. Twenty feet in front of him was a group meeting and working on a project, and lo and behold, they were having Papa John's pizza. He closed his eyes and tried not to inhale too much. Within ten minutes, they were finished, and most of them left. One of the students spoke to him, and he opened his eyes. The guy was standing with a Papa John's pizza box, and he said, "Listen, we ordered two pizzas, thinking we were going to be here longer, but we finished early, and we don't want to throw this away, having spent money for it, so if you want it, you can have it."

Trim replied, "Yeah, sure, and thanks."

And guess what? Inside the box was a whole pizza. It was a hand-tossed pizza that was made just like how he liked it. Trim went into the bathroom and cried in stealth mode—not just because of the pizza but because God was showing him that He was with him and would feed him the same way He fed Elijah in the wilderness, David when he was on the run from King Saul, Paul when he was shipwrecked, and John when he was on the island of Patmos. The fire that he got from the thought that God loved, cared, and provided for him like he did those Bible greats melted the ice of his doubt, and the water flowed through his eyes and dripped onto the palms of his hands. Trim knew it could only have been God, for he had a better chance of winning the lottery five days in a row than for that to happen. There he was—hungry, disappointed, and uncertain—with a mere thought in the form of a desire for food, and it materialized into not only sustenance but also trust for God. He had moved from having faith to believing and from just believing to trusting, and that in and of itself changed his life forever and was worth every tear. Boy, I just get choked up while thinking about it. At forty-six years old, on June 14, 1997, he graduated with his momma and sister, among others, looking on. He was told that he was the second person in GA Tech history to receive a bachelor's degree past the age of forty. God is real, my friend, and He is not just a theological concept. But it gets even better.

Later on, Trim wrote the president of GA Tech to make him aware of this and other events involving Tech that were part of the saga of his life.

Now let's talk about Ms. Cobb. After four interviews, Capital One recruited Trim to come work for them as a network analyst in Richmond, Virginia. They offered him a ten-thousand-dollar signing bonus, which he gracefully accepted. After a few months, Capital One and Trim parted ways, but not before he met and fell in love with Annie, a program analyst. They were together for eight years. Annie, who was a widow, had two daughters, and Trim treated them like they were his own. He was the only father figure that they knew of since their dad died when they were very young. Trim had been working for LMR (Logistics Management Resources) in Prince George, Virginia, and on his lunch hour, he would go to Southside Hospital in Petersburg to volunteer. What could he do in one hour or less? Having compassion for people, he thought about all the people who were in the hospital and rarely had visitors, if any at all. So during his paydays, he would stop by a florist and buy flowers and take them to the strangers he would visit and spend some time with. Little did he know that such a thing would change his life profoundly. No one knew he was doing this except the volunteer department at the hospital. He always sought to make a positive difference in the lives of others, and perhaps that's why he stuck by Annie and the kids as long as he did. As the girls got older, they began to have an appetite for boys, and Trim was very protective of them. Did I not say that he treated them like his own? The older one, a master manipulator, began to drive a wedge between him and Annie in order to have her way. The fire in their relationship began to dwindle, and he felt very sad because he was unable to resolve things. The older daughter was making Annie choose between her and him. No one knows the despair of a soldier who fights a war he knows he cannot win.

One morning, on his way to work, Trim began to weep profusely. He felt unloved and unappreciated. He asked God to take away those feelings. It was a payday, so at lunchtime, he went to Southside and went to the volunteer office with a dozen long-stem roses. As usual, the person in charge gave him a room number and a name, so he went on his way to make a difference. He entered the room, and there, lying on the bed, was a Caucasian female in her late seventies or early eighties. She was wearing a pair of wraparound sunglasses similar to the ones optometrists give you when you get your eyes dilated. He introduced himself and gave her the roses. They spent twenty or thirty minutes getting to know one another, and then it was time for him to go. Before making his exit, she called him over to her bedside. He thought she might have wanted him to fix her pillow or further elevate her bed. Instead, she reached up and pulled him toward her with both of her hands grasping his cheeks. And then she rose up gently and gingerly placed a kiss on his forehead before saying "Thank you." Something just went all over him as he realized that it was God answering his prayer. Her name was Ms. Cobb, and they became wonderful friends. He visited her three weeks in a row. He received a call at work from her daughter; she thanked him for making a difference in her mother's life. During one of the visits, he discovered that Ms. Cobb loved Hershey's chocolate bars. Before going to the hospital on his third visit, he stopped by a store and bought a giant Hershey bar; it was about three feet long and two feet wide. She was eagerly looking forward to his visit, to say the least. After arriving at her room, he stuck his head inside the door and asked her to close her eyes and to stretch out her arms. He entered and placed the giant bar in her arms. After opening her eyes, she just cried. They both did, as a matter of fact. The following week, his job took him out of town, so he didn't visit. Upon his return, he went to see her and discovered that she had been transferred to a nursing home a few miles away. Trim returned to work, for he didn't have time to find the place. The next day, at lunchtime, after discovering the location of the home, he ventured out to see his friend. When he got there at around 12:15 p.m., he went to her room, and it was empty. He went to the desk to ask for where she was. Well, they had moved her but not before God did, for she died at around 10:00 a.m. I won't even try to describe how he felt or what he went through. Her daughter contacted him about two weeks later and asked him to come by her dress boutique as she had something for him. He was delighted to meet with her but not as elated as he was to receive a photo of Ms. Cobb and an engraved silver pillbox that belonged to her. He took her personal possessions back to the office and erected a shrine of his friend on his desk. He has never forgotten her because she was more than a friend for a short period; she was a reminder of God's compassion for him and one of Yahweh's many provisions.

I know you want to connect the dots here in order to make some sense of what my point must be and what I'm getting at because it seems like I'm just ramblin' on and on. So let me help you out a bit. He told me, "All of this has to do with God's provision." The Bible says in 1 Corinthians 2:9, "But as it is written, Eye hath not seen, nor ear heard, neither have entered into the heart of man, the things which **God hath prepared** for them that love him." When Abraham was told to sacrifice Isaac, God had already prepared a sacrifice in the form of a ram so that Abraham could obey God and move on to the next level. He promised him three things—a homeland, a heritage, and an heir, and so it is with us also. Our Heavenly Father sees all and knows all. He knows what we need, and He, through His love and the keeping of His Word, has prepared a "ram" to meet our needs and stored it somewhere. First, all we have to do is simply believe that. Then we must trust in God and His Word. Once you do that, then you have to ask God for where He left your provision. He will dispatch an angel and/or the Holy Spirit to lead and/or guide you to where He left it for you. I ain't telling you something I read. I'm telling you something that I *know*! You'd be surprised by the amount of Christians who believe in God but still don't trust him. Trusting in God seems to be optional when it comes to salvation. Just as humans have stages of development, so does the Spirit. When we are infants in Christ, we have faith. As adolescents in Christ, we have belief, and when we no longer need milk and can digest meat, we then have trust. The growth of too many believers is stunted because they fail to move to the next level of their relationship with God. You hear a lot of people say that trust is the most important part of a relationship, but they never include or think about that when it comes to their relationship with God.

You see, because Trim trusted in God, he was provided a means to keep his word to his dad and finish GA Tech. It was his trust in God that provided the bail money. It was his trust in God that provided him the Papa John's pizza just the way he liked it. It was his trust in God that provided Dr. Adler, who used his influence to get him a place to stay and two part-time jobs on campus; When you think of the ten-thousand-dollar signing bonus, it was trust that was responsible for it. I forgot to tell you that when he got to Richmond, Capital One put him in a luxurious, furnished apartment for sixty days and provided him with a rental car. He told me that when that happened, what came to his mind was 1 Corinthians 2:9: "But as it is written, Eye hath not seen, nor ear heard, neither have entered into the heart of man, the things which God hath prepared for them that love him." He remembered Philippians 4:19 as well: "But my God shall supply all your need according to his riches in glory by Christ Jesus." Finally, it was trust that provided Ms. Cobb when he was at one of the lowest places of his journey. He said to me that God will perform His Word in your life even more when you learn to trust him. I discovered that Trim had been up for four days straight in order to study for his final exams, and the last one was physics, which he had not studied for due to exhaustion. But he prayed and trusted in God, and even though he didn't get an A or even a B, he did score enough to pass. It was *trust* that provided Madelyn, who fed and nursed him back to health when he was sick in a foreign country with no family or insurance. There's a lot to be said about that trust thing. Shucks, he even got me to think about what I had been doing wrong in my relationship with God. I'm not trying to preach to ya. What I am trying to do is demonstrate and show to you that not only is God real and that He will perform His Word in our lives if we trust Him but also that He loves us enough to leave provisions for us so we can move to the next level of our spiritual development and relationship with Him. The kicker is trust because it is the key that unlocks the door of the place that stores the provisions of God, which are vouchsafed and sealed for His children. You have to understand that we are all creatures of God, but not all of us are children of God.

All this time we've been climbing the mountain, and now it's time to go to the summit. Are you ready? Well, sir, it's like this: God will *always provide*:

- God will always provide a means for us to obey Him, to escape the snares of Satan, and to move to the next level.
- God will always provide a means for us to move out of our captivity at the appointed time by parting our situations and/or circumstances like the Red Sea.
- God will always provide a means for us to accomplish the things He has ordained and called for us to do.
- God will always provide, and we have to ask God our Father where he left the provision; although we should never question God, He is always delighted for us to ask Him a question (and there is a difference—one that a wise man knows and a fool does not). We have to learn to ask God where He left the provision and to send us help from on high. We have to ask Him to lead us to the provision *while preparing us for the provision*. I will say here that many of us want the blessing but are not prepared to receive the blessing. If David had become the king of Israel on the spot when Samuel anointed him, he wouldn't have had the character and insight necessary to remain king; God had to prepare him. It's one thing

to get the position and another thing to keep it. God will not set us up to fail; therefore, He will prepare us for the blessing so we don't end up destroying ourselves and/or others with it. Maybe God hasn't answered your prayer because you're *not ready to receive the blessing.*

- When it comes to the provision, God will not only meet but also may exceed your expectation based on the level of your trust in Him. We know He's able, and it is our trust in Him that seems to also make Him willing.

- The provision might be a person, place, thing, attitude, epiphany, ministering spirit, or revelation. The provision can take the form of a means of escape from death, poverty, persecution, and even damnation. The provision can be an answer to an important and pertinent question. The provision can come in many different forms.

- Sometimes we become the provision when we're open and willing to be used by God, but we must make ourselves available and accessible. Whatever we do, we must remember that *God allows us to do it so that He will be glorified while others are blessed,* for we truly are our brothers' keepers.

- God is God, not a genie. He does not spoil His children like so many parents do, which results in their demise and destruction. Perhaps you're without the provision because you do not first seek the kingdom of God and His righteousness but rather fame, riches, and self-gratification, being a pleaser of men and self rather than a pleaser of God. Matthew 6:33 says, "But seek ye first the kingdom of God, and his righteousness; and all these things shall be added unto you."

Well, young fella', it's been real, but I gotta go, so I'm applying the brakes now so you can get out because I gotta go hang out with Trim a while and listen some more as he reads me excerpts from his autobiography entitled *So Much Left Unsaid.* He's quite an interesting fella'. You should meet him sometime. Bye now. Gotta go. Thanks for not cuttin' the cheese, and please don't slam my truck door while getting' out. Uncle Ned will catch you later.

The End

PS: I almost forgot the copy of the letter, so here it is.

Subject: Letter concerning Dr. Philip Adler
To: Dr. George Bud Peterson
Date: Tuesday, May 12, 2015, 11:16 PM

Dr. Peterson,

I'm writing you this letter to acquaint you with things behind the scenes when it comes to historical and humanitarian events involving GA Tech that you otherwise would not know. Let me begin by introducing myself. I am Larry D. Mance of Toccoa, GA (all my friends know me as "Skeeter" which is my pen name as well). Myself, my brother, first cousin and 6 other Blacks integrated public schools in 1965 in Toccoa (Stephens County) GA for the first time in the history of this country. For two years being the only Black in all my 6 classes, no one talked to me, sat by me and not even the teachers would recognize me whenever I held up my hand to participate in class. Attached is a short story from my book "Teachable Moments" (an e-book sold on Amazon.com) and it talks about when I first came to Atlanta with my sister for Christmas vacation at age 10 yrs old seeing the round building at GA Tech (the first one I'd ever seen). I asked my sister what it was and she said "That's GA Tech. You're gonna' go there one day" It meant nothing to me then but I graduated high school in 1969 and started GA Tech March of 1970 becoming the first Black American in the history of Northeast Georgia to ever enter GA Tech (and not by athletic scholarship but purely academics working full time while going to school full time).

Now I will get to my point. In my sophomore year I fell in love got married and dropped out of Tech vowing to one day finish. After all my kids were grown and emancipated in 1995 I sought to fulfill that vow. But the head of the school of MGT. (Dr. Lloyd Byers) refused to let me back in. I appealed to the vice president of Academic affairs as I had never flunked out of Tech (a promise I made to Dr. Roper who allowed me entry relaxing the "Black Quota" requirement back in Jan. 1970). The vice president said that Dr. Byers felt I didn't want a degree from Tech since I had withdrawn so many times over the years. I explained that the record would show that I had no student loan(s) as I worked full time and went to school full time until I ran out of money as Tech was not going to let me go for free. I would save money and go back for a class or two until I got my credits down to where I only needed 30 credit hours to graduate. Dr. Byars said he would let me back in but only by applying the ten year rule; consequently I lost 60 credit hours. But I got down on my knees after pulling that arrow out of my chest and re-enrolled June of 1995. I was married for the second time by then and 6 months before graduating we had our problems and she placed all my belongings on the curb. I had and drove a 1961 Volvo (PV 544) which I slept in the student center parking lot washing up in the men's bathroom but never missing a class for I was bound and determined not to let anything keep me from succeeding. Being homeless, jobless and hungry for a little more than 3 weeks, Dr. Adler discovered my dilemma and condition and went to the President of Tech and told them what was happening with me and asked if there was an empty room somewhere on campus that Tech could let me have so I could finish. GA Tech gave me a vacant room in the International Students Dorm and then helped me get 2 part time jobs on campus so I could eat, pay my fees and have money to fund my class projects in order to graduate. I drove the Stinger (shuttle) and I worked on PCs and installed voice recognition software (in its experimental stages) for paraplegics throughout the city as a part of a research grant Tech had been given. On June the 14th 1997 I finished all requirements and graduated with a job waiting for me as a Network Analyst for Capital One that paid me a $10K signing bonus resulting from Dr. Adler's recommendation. Although I am a 100% service connected disabled veteran (Vietnam Era Ex-Air Force) having Agent Orange exposure I have a lot of health problems but amnesia is not one of them. And while I'm living I remember The Dr. Adlers, The Dr. Ropers, Dr. Sherman Dallas's, Edith Blicksilvers, Dr. Charles Liottas (another one of my mentors) and GA Tech in general and I say thank you. My dad will turn 101 yrs old on the 30th of May (still driving and cutting grass) and I promised him that I would not let getting married at 20 yrs old keep me from finishing Tech. I have learned that no one is successful on their own as somebody somewhere had to help them whether they deserved it or not. All mentioned in this letter fit that category but none so great as Dr. Adler. One last thing, Capital One took me through 4 sets of Interviews. The second time they sent a team of 5 managers from Richmond to the Ritz Carlton. Around 11 AM while going from suite to suite a manager asked me something outside the box. He asked me "Who are your heroes?" I said to him "Sir my heroes are first of all my father, second Dr. Philip Adler and third Dr. Charles Liotta. My heroes are not the Jessie Jackson's or the Michael Jordan's (men's whose hands I may never shake or faces I may never see); But rather these men who have invested a part of their lives in me." And on that note I will close. I feel that such great men need to be recognized by the seeds they've sown as well as the fields where they've sown them. I hope you will give Dr. Adler a plaque, a trophy and, at the very least, a phone call having some recognition for what he's accomplished beyond the paycheck, the expectation and beyond the call of duty. If we had more men like these, there would be no Fergusons, Tulsas or Baltimores neither would China ever be a world threat.

With Regards and Respect,
Larry "Skeeter" Mance

The Smallest Wrestler

It was 1965—when public schools in the South integrated under the Freedom of Choice plan—and for the very first time in the history of this country, blacks and whites sat in the same classroom. Darien, Georgia, found itself to be part of a social experiment that sought to prove that blacks were inferior to whites and could not compete with them academically. Quan, a Geech, was an aspiring wrestler. He was stocky but not fat and a descendant of the Gullah. He was five feet four and vertically challenged for his weight class. He was one of nine black Americans who "crossed the tracks"; they broke the color barrier. It was high time for the South to dismantle the "separate but equal" system—one that was indeed separate but never equal. He, like many other blacks in the rural South, searched for an education as his father could not read or write and his mother could barely do those things. Among other things, he was a high school teenager and adventurous/curious; he craved notoriety, popularity, and a state wrestling championship. Being the grandson of a proud gandy dancer, Quan always sought to soar above mediocrity by not simply meeting the expectation but exceeding it. There were many things that he excelled in, but wrestling, his passion, was not one of them—at least, not at the moment. Did I fail to mention that he was the only black in all his classes for the first two years of high school and that for the very first time in his life, he got a brand spanking new textbook? Yes, for the first time since he started school, he had books with the most current information rather than ones that were ten years obsolete and missing pages.

Quan, known as the Punisher, was fast. He was also known as a hard trier as no one tried as hard as he did at anything. He had a slogan—"Failure is not an option." His African heritage could not be traced, but somewhere down the line, he must've had some Zulu in him, for he was cunning, thorough, and without fear. He just couldn't seem to win most of his matches. It did not matter that he was the invisible man because in his first two years of high school, no one sat by him, talked to him, or recognized him; his teachers wouldn't even call him whenever he raised his hand in an effort to participate in class during his freshman and sophomore days. Still, he represented and gained the respect and admiration of his teammates and coach. He was brought up in the church and refused to allow the threads of racial hatred to make up the fabric of his character. He realized at an early age that the true test of *Christian love* involves not only loving those who love you but also loving those who don't! His convictions wouldn't allow him to hate, for he refused to let the bad in others change the good in him. He always sought to be greater (though not better) by choosing to forgive the racists who taunted him with racial slurs and threats. If that wasn't enough, He also had to battle previous schoolmates in his own community when they ostracized him for "going to school with white folk." It was a difficult time in America, and racial hatred flared up on both sides. He remembered what his mother, Millie, always said about conflict: "Somebody's gotta have some sense." What she meant was that people have to learn to step outside themselves—their pride, their erroneous teachings, and even their comfort zones—in order to objectively consider the outcome of a thought, idea, behavior, or action.

Perhaps his desire to wrestle came from the Bible story of Jacob, whose name was changed to Israel after he wrestled with the angel, for it indeed had a great influence on his life. But more than that, he embraced and treasured the concepts of forgiveness and reconciliation (two things that we all seem to wrestle with at some point in our lives), realizing we're all God's creations and none of us are perfect save for Christ Himself. He often recalled his grandmother saying, "We're all God's creatures, but we're not all God's children." Both his Christianity and his character were put to the test on a daily basis at his school and at his home. He could put his hands on his opponent inside the wrestling circle, but grabbing hold of acceptance and understanding in his world/life was a different foe that oftentimes flipped and tossed him at will against the walls of his mind. Sometimes he would lose control and forget who he was in the Lord, letting his anger cause him to sin by disliking the person rather than their behavior. He would have to remind himself that God hates the sin but not the sinner, and that thought became the compass needle that pointed toward spiritual freedom.

It was the beginning of his junior year when he sat down and talked with his grandmother (an old saint who knew how to get a prayer answered) about his goal and dream. No one knew how old she was. She was born during the time when blacks were considered chattel and not allowed birth certificates; however, she could remember back 104 years. He told her how he was determined to win a state championship and asked her for her advice. She asked him if he prayed before his matches, and he replied no. She told him that, from what she could see, he was making two big mistakes. "First of all," she said, "God wants to be first and foremost. The Bible says, 'Thou shall have no other gods before me [Exodus 20:3]' and 'Thou shalt love the Lord thy God with all thine heart, and with all thy soul, and with all thy might [Deuteronomy 6:5].' That's what 'first and foremost' means. By not praying before your matches, you're not making him first and foremost. You're making the match first and foremost instead. Then it says, 'Create in me a clean heart, O God; and renew a right spirit within me [Psalms 51:10].' That has to do with the motive inside your heart. Do you want a championship so that God will be glorified in your testimony, or is it because of your ego, pride, and desire to be a big shot? Do you want it so all the little girls will run after you? Is it for God's glory, or is it for your swag?"

Quan was knocked back by his grandmother's counsel. The word of God echoed throughout the canyons of his thoughts. He walked home with her words ringing in his thoughts like church bells on Easter Sunday; they were edifying seeds of wisdom that had to be reckoned with.

That night, Quan prayed a special prayer. He asked God to search his heart, his soul, and his mind and to help him do the right thing, at the right time, in the right way, for the right reason, and with the right one. He asked God to help him walk before Him in such a way that it would cause His heart to smile rather than frown; additionally, he asked God to remove anything that He found unpleasing in His sight. After falling asleep for about two hours, a visitor awakened Quan, and it was not his mother, to say the least. The molecules in the air seemed to sparkle around the divine visitor. He was the most beautiful creature Quan had ever seen—so beautiful that he looked as if he had been carved out of the very air—and he had bright light emanating from his profile. He introduced himself as Uriel, one of the Archangels that forever stand before the presence of Almighty God. Uriel told him that Christ himself dispatched him after placing Quan's sincere prayer in the lap of the Father. Uriel said, "God has a purpose for everything He does and says. Whatever He gives us has a two-fold purpose—whether it is a talent, skill, money, property, or whatever. The first part of it is that He will be glorified, and the second part is that others will be blessed." He said that Quan should bear witness to those who might be lost around him. Quan should tell them that God is real and that He answers prayers and that He loves us and wants the best for us and that He has feelings like you and me. Sometimes we think that God does not feel, but how can that be if He "so loved the world" or if "it repented God in His heart." He told Quan that he should awake thirty minutes early every day with the intent of doing nothing more than communicating with God; This communication should focus on listening to God rather than talking to him, for we are taught to pray but not to listen to Him. Many of us want to hear from God, but we spend no time making the effort to listen to God. The way we do that is we turn off the television, the radio, the laptop, and the telephone and tell God, "Here I am, Lord. Speak to me. And if you have nothing to say, then just let me feel your presence, allowing me to fellowship with you." In the presence of God, there is *peace*, there is *power*, and there is *prosperity*! Unless one is born deaf, one has the ability to hear, but *listening* is a skill we have to learn to develop. Someone once said, "You'll know when you've learned how to listen not when you can hear what's said, but, rather, whenever you can hear what's not said." Think about that one real hard.

Quan obeyed Uriel's instructions the next morning, and a strange sensation came over him. His arteries and veins seemed to be dammed up yet exploding with love that was abounding inside him, overflowing into every thought, every feeling, and every fiber of his being—so much that his heart felt enlarged with unspeakable joy that crested out of his eyelids and rolled down his cheeks. He found himself weeping. Although he had cried many times before in his life, this was the first time he cried because of joy rather than sorrow, and he knew that he was being filled with the Holy Spirit. He began to perspire but the odd thing was that his perspiration was more oily than wet. Even though he wanted to stay there in that moment of time, he knew that school was calling and that he had his first match of the season later that evening. At the beginning of the school year, two guys, David and Alex, broke the Southern racial code by befriending Quan. They noticed something different about him that they could not dissect or analyze, for he, Quan, walked with a new confidence, spoke with a new tone, smiled a new smile, and exuded some kind of peace that was beyond their comprehension and understanding. Little did they know that Quan had received power from on high! It's impossible to encounter the throne of God and remain the same. Whatever it was, they wanted it too, but both were reluctant and too afraid to ask him for the source of his change.

But this was a special day, for it was the beginning of the wrestling season, and Quan's match was the last one. The opposing team was new to the conference because of the redistricting that had occurred. Now they were Quan's school schedule. They were bigger, tougher, and more experienced and had been the state champs for three years in a row. Eleven of Quan's teammates had their turns on the mats, and none of them won their matches. The school and coach were afraid that it was going to be a complete shutout. Quan was up next, and he began to sweat like he never sweated before, but the only thing he was afraid of was that his antiperspirant might not hold up. He constantly said in his mind, "I can do all things through Christ who strengthens me [Philippians 4:13]." The bleachers were overflowing with students, parents, teachers, and siblings; they contained just about the whole town except for Quan's parents, who had to work. Nonetheless, Quan understood their sacrifice and always tried to bring honor to their heads. The commentator announced Quan's match from the sidelines, and Quan was taken aback by his opponent's enormity. Surely there had to be some mistake, for this was a high school wrestling match, not the Philistine battlefield where David fought Goliath with Quan now acting as David's stand-in. Oh, baby! This was going to be one for the records, and it was gonna be on like Donkey Kong. Quan thought, *It's a good thing I already said my prayers 'cause this guy is gonna kill me, and I might not get the chance to pray before I die.* The whistle blew, and the match was on.

The mammoth wrestler grabbed Quan. I can't say if it was out of fear, reflex, or instinct, but when he could not get a grip, Quan sidestepped him like greased lightning before flipping him onto the mat, looping his arm around his neck, and placing him in a choke hold. He almost got disqualified for nearly putting him to sleep as Quan was afraid to let "Paul Bunyan" go after the referee had made the count and blew the whistle. Now there were just two more bouts to go. Again the whistle blew. After having been both angered and embarrassed, Quan's opponent fouled him and won the round; the referee refused to call the foul even though Quan's coach and teammates protested animatedly. But Quan remained focused, sweating oil instead of salt, and his hands and fingers felt like Velcro. When the whistle blew, Quan was all over his opponent, dodging his lunges like he was

Neo from *The Matrix*. Then all of a sudden, to the crowd's surprise, Quan moved like a mongoose fighting against a cobra and somehow ended up putting the guy in an arm bar, forcing him to submit. The auditorium went berserk. People were running and screaming. Paper and popcorn were flying. Quan and his teammates were jumping around like canecutters because Quan had prevented a shutout. As the noise began to die down, Quan heard a loud voice from the stands say, "That'll break dat dog from sucking eggs," and he knew instinctively that it was his grandmother. But before he could look up, he heard, "If you can't run wid the big dogs, then you need to stay on the porch. Don't you bring yo' big self down here no moe, thinkin' you can whip my son." Looking up, Quan saw his mom and dad, who came to see him for the first time. This was a day of days and one that Quan, the Punisher, would never forget.

That night, after Quan said his prayers and fell asleep, Uriel returned. He told Quan that he was becoming a stigmata and that his sweat was mixed with oil because of the anointing of the Holy Spirit. He informed Quan that God was preparing him for a mission. He told Quan that a third of the angels fell and were cast out for making the wrong choice—siding with Satan. Currently, less than 10 percent of all mankind acknowledge that there is a God, that there was a creation, and that Christ (the promised Messiah) came and will return. Too many don't believe that Heaven and Hell are real places. He encouraged Quan to change his handle, for "as a man thinketh in his heart, so is he" (Proverbs 23:7). Before leaving, he reminded Quan to always put God first and make Him foremost in his life and to never allow hatred, greed, malice, and all the other sins of the spirit to enter his life. Quan then asked him a question. "What does God want?"

Uriel said, "From the very first word of Genesis to the very last word of Revelation, the whole Bible can be summed up in just one sentence: *God wants to have a relationship with you and with me!* For God so loved man that he created a plan of salvation as a means for redemption whereby He might be able to have an eternal relationship with all men and women, boys and girls, children and adults. There is no plan of salvation or redemption for angels, and that is one of the reasons why Satan hates mankind so much and is determined to destroy all that God loves. Your grandmother was right. We might all be creatures of God, but not all of us are children of God."

Uriel said, "Your opponents are indicative of Satan and the fallen. 'For we wrestle not against flesh and blood, but against principalities, against powers, against the rulers of the darkness of this world, against spiritual wickedness in high places [Ephesians 6:12].' And the only way to defeat them is through the power of the Holy Spirit. The opponents are but demonic attacks sent to defeat all the baptized believers by subduing and controlling them through spiritual pressure points and choke holds, causing them to submit, give up, and become defeated. Oftentimes, we blame God and think that He's supposed to save us because we asked Him to. But He has already made provisions for our victory through the anointing of the Holy Spirit. When the oil of anointing flows upon a man or woman and they oil up with the Holy Spirit, Satan cannot grip, grab, or grapple with that person, for they slip right out from under his attacks, leaving them *unaffected and noninfected.* They become like Teflon when Satan and his minions throw attacks their way. They—the situations, circumstances, illnesses, or whatever—might hit the person, but then they just slide right off, leaving them unharmed but stronger. The Holy Spirit causes you to succeed against all odds not because of whom you are but because of whom Christ is. The Holy Spirit allows you to take the authority over the enemy, empowering you to tear down strongholds and set captives free. You are no match for Satan and his fallen angels and evil spirits. Therefore, you need power from on high to subdue him. The Holy Spirit is the exerciser of that power, and He will work through us if we allow ourselves to be used as vessels of the throne of God and become conduits of His power. Jesus told the disciples after the resurrection to tarry in the upper room until the Holy Spirit came so that they might receive power. Never forget that we have no power except what God gives or loans to us. He structured it that way to keep us humble lest anyone would become arrogant and attempt to assert themselves like Peter did while he was walking on water or King Saul did when he did not slay all the Amalekites or Pharaoh did when he thought that he was a god. But you have to be washed in the blood before the anointing will come or flow. A person usually applies oil or moisturizer after a bath so the surface area will be clean before the application. It's the same way when it comes to the anointing of the Holy Spirit. First, we must be clean (i.e., washed in the blood of the Lamb), and then the oil of anointing can be easily applied to us. If Satan attacks us through demonic influences, the unseen forces of evil will be left impotent, taking us out of the 'match of living life rather than surviving it.' Living life is totally opposite of surviving life. The good thing is that Christ has given us the authority to choke-hold the enemy, but it is the Holy Spirit that exercises through us the power necessary to carry out the mandate to tear down the strongholds and set the captives free. With the anointing present in your life, the enemy cannot harm you. He will always attack you but to no avail. Before the enemy was once like a pterodactyl. Now, by the presence and power of the Holy Spirit, he is like a mosquito."

Quan told Uriel that many of his friends at church were saying that the Bible is not accurate and is comprised merely of stories that aren't real and are not to be taken literally. "They say that the way the Bible was put together by the Council of Nicaea made it full of flaws. Because of the politics that occurred within the council, the truth was compromised."

To this, Uriel responded, "The believer has to accept the Bible as the infallible word of God and believe it is true in its entirety—from the first word of Genesis to the last word of Revelation. No other book in the world can make that claim. Although there may be books missing that perhaps should have been included, God ordained it, so what is there is enough. There are things like the Dead Sea Scrolls, computers, the Books of Enoch, etc., that He has reserved for the end-time— things that were not intended to be uncovered during the time the Bible was being bound. But that does not take away from the fact that what is bound between the covers is true. 'God is not a man, that he should lie; neither the son of man, that he should repent: hath he said, and shall he not do it? or hath he spoken, and shall he not make it good?' (Numbers 23:19). One should never question God or stop asking Him questions. It's one thing to question God and another thing to ask Him a question."

Saturday, the next day, Quan went to his grandmother's to share with her the events that unfolded the night before. Although she was awed, she was not surprised, for divine visitors had come to visit her in the middle of the night too in the past. Quan told her that he was going to change his handle from the Punisher to the Ferryman. When she asked him why, he simply said, "I realize that my purpose is not to punish my fellow men but to ferry them to the foot of the cross, where they might meet the Lord Jesus Christ and thereby make a decision to accept Him as the Savior and have a relationship with Jah (Almighty God the Father and the Creator of all there is and all there'll ever be)." That year, Quan went on to be undefeated, exceeding expectations, winning his bouts against all odds, and capturing a state championship. But the best part is that the championship allowed him to become influential; it helped him introduce many of his teammates and friends to Christ, who became their personal Savior. He continues to ferry young people, strangers, and associates to the foot of the cross to this very day.

The End

Too Busy Being Busy

(Based on a True Story)

It was a critical time in his life—a time when he needed someone to listen to him, to believe him, and to celebrate rather than tolerate him, but as fate would have it, it was not to be had. His mother returned to work when he was two weeks old, and his sister (who was twelve years older than him) became his surrogate mom. She taught him how to spell his first word at age 3 (i.e., *cow*) and to read at age 4. By the time he started kindergarten at age 5, he could write his ABCs and his name and knew his address. She gave him his first and only birthday party as a child, making him a coconut cake that used a banana fashioned into a man with arms and legs and pieces of cherries that acted as the man's eyes and mouth. And she was beautiful; she was black American and Cherokee. Her hair reached the floor whenever she sat in a straight-backed chair, and he and his nineteen-month-old brother fought over who would comb it. They envisioned a horse's mane as they pulled the comb slowly past her beautiful skin, which housed not one pimple or blackhead. She was beautiful and as "fine as frog's hair." Her complexion was as black as an African in the Congo sun, and he loved her dearly.

She was the first person in her family to not only finish high school but also attend college. He remembered the many times when he accompanied his mother to see her at Fort Valley State College in Georgia, where they kept a huge alligator chained beside a fifty-five-gallon oil drum that was cut in half and filled with water. He was rejected by his dad, his brother, and his peers/classmates but was never rejected by his sister. His mom worked so hard to support the family that she never had time for him, and his dog(s) filled the void. When his sister would come home for the summer, she would work all day—ironing, cooking, cleaning, and caring for him and his brother. He loved her so much that he would go out to the yard or slip across the street to go to the vacant lot and make a bouquet of wildflowers for her. He used to say to her as he presented to her the flowers, "Sister, when I grow up, I'm gonna marry you." He was only a child; he knew nothing about the incest laws that would prevent such a thing. All he knew was the love he had for his sister, and he wanted her to always be in his life.

A major crisis erupted when after she graduated, a guy showed up one day and asked for her hand in marriage. Her bags were already packed, and her mind was already made up, so you could imagine her parents' reaction to this stranger who wanted to marry and take away their daughter. He recalled how his world spun out of control and how his cowardly older brother acted out by trying to kill himself with a butter knife. He thought to himself, *Who are you trying to fool with a butter knife? Anybody can see you're faking it, fool! Ray Charles, Jose Feliciano, and Stevie Wonder are all blind, but even they can see that!* He did not know what to do, and the vacuum that was created in his life by her absence could only be matched by the hole that was now in his heart. Several years after she got married, the sister came home to pick up her baby brothers and take them to the big city of Atlanta for Christmas. She believed that the key to them becoming successful in life depended on their early educational exposure to new horizons and frontiers that would provide positive experiences beyond what a small mountain town could offer. As the brand-new 1961 fire-engine-red Chevrolet Corvair ferried them from the mountains to the city, a spectacular thing happened. Over the years, his sister's theory would prove to be correct. One would be hard-pressed to explain what all the neon lights, decorations, tall buildings, and sheer vastness did to the minds and eyes of those two little boys, who were now ten and twelve years old. I must say that this sister wasn't just a good sister; she was a *great* sister!

As they were entering the city, off to the right was a huge round building—the first round building he had ever seen. Standing up in the back seat, he touched his sister (who was sitting on the passenger side) and asked, "Sister, what's that?"

She replied, "That's Georgia Tech. One day, you're going to go to college there."

He did not understand the significance of her words. *Jim Crow*, *segregation*, and *separate-but-equal* were meaningless to him as they were terms that did not reside in his vocabulary. He was a child, and a child doesn't know hatred or see color until some adult comes along and installs it into their way of thinking like a computer virus that spreads throughout their entire life. He realized that neither he nor any black person he knew could sit in a restaurant in his sleepy little town, and that's why his mother always made him eat before she took him with her to the town to buy him shoes, shirts, pants, and so forth. At the train station, the water fountains and restrooms were labeled Colored and White, but the reason for such labels never dawned on him. He didn't know that a black person had never studied at Tech; he just knew it was a big school that had a cool round building. As fate would have it, he became the first minority in the history of his town and the northeastern Georgia region to enroll in Georgia Tech (the Harvard of the South) all because of the seed his sister planted that day.

He always made sure that he remembered his sister's birthday every year and even remembered his brother's and parents' birthdays even though they never remembered his. No one can imagine the pain that a child feels when his parents are so busy with work or doing whatever that they don't even remember the day he entered the world, but he bore it silently with tears that cascaded over his soul like an underground river that never surfaced. Everybody was either too busy being busy or just didn't care. The Cherokee in him made him strong and able to bear the pain. He showed no sign of it because he was taught that men didn't cry, and he came into this world as a man.

He always wanted to make his parents proud of him, so he sought to excel in everything he did. His father only completed the second grade and couldn't read or write; his mother completed the sixth grade and could read and write a little. He was a straight A student and won many awards, but there was never anyone from his family who saw him receive them. He won second place in the state's spelling bee when he was in the fourth grade, and when he was in the sixth grade, the high school principal came to him and asked him to represent the school in the state's oration contest. He recalled his mother buying him a new suit for the occasion and writing his speech on "The Utilization of One's Resources." He was the youngest person competing; he was only eleven years old, and the other contestants were between fifteen years to eighteen years old. When it was his turn to go to the microphone, he stood up, and while tugging the end of his coat, he marched to the mic. He paused before beginning his speech not because of stage fright but to look at all the people in the bleachers of the high school auditorium—the mothers, fathers, siblings, and cousins who came to support the other participants; there was nobody there for him because everybody he knew was too busy being busy.

Many things happened as the years went by—some good and some bad—but a good thing never came without a struggle because always between the promise and the prize is the problem. He learned at an early age that before he could receive the prize, he had to endure and overcome the problem Perhaps God designed it that way for him to learn and understand that he could do nothing without Christ; for that, he was thankful, for he discovered the missing ingredient and key to success at an early age. As time went on, he made an effort to spend time with his sister, but she was always busy. Their mother had contracted Alzheimer's several years before her death, and the sister assumed the responsibilities the mother had. She would take a two-hour drive to their home from Atlanta to do the cooking, the washing, the shopping, the banking, and so forth. Having to run two households and her church duties stretched the sister out. She did not have time for herself, let alone her baby brother, and it grieved him severely that she never went on a vacation; she rarely went out to dinner and was always busy being busy. They used to spend time together by gleaning the Scriptures rightly and dividing the Word, but now she was too tired to entertain such a thing. He mourned her for she seemed to be someone who was dead but hadn't been buried yet. The brother kept trying to spend time with her, but she was too busy. He thought about writing her a letter, but she would be too busy to take the time to read it because she was too busy being busy.

After a while, she became a reprobate. She thought she was doing right while doing wrong; she thought she was pleasing God but was too busy to spend time with Him. As she got older and reached her senior years, she became very busy with doing various things. She became ineffective because she spread herself too thin and her energy became unfocused. She did not realize that the enemy had sent a busy demon to plague and encircle her. She had become busy with being busy. It got to the point where her walk with God was affected, for she was too busy to spend time alone with Him. Sure, she always prayed, but God wants to be heard more than talked to. God had sent a messenger to her, but because she was so busy, she didn't have the time to listen to the messenger. She became like a dog that chases its own tail—busy with going around in circles. She was too busy to become enlightened, too busy to become awakened, too busy to feel His presence, and too busy for the scales to fall from her eyes so she might see the things God has hidden from the eyes of man.

Alas, she was too busy to consider that. In the West Indies, they have an expression: "Sometimes you have to take the time to take the time." This means there are some things that one has to *make* time for—like spending time with God.

In Exodus 20:1–3 is the first commandment of the eleven (ten were given to Moses, and one was given by Christ). God said, "Thou shalt have no other god before me," and He went on to warn the Israelites about worshiping idols. An idol can be tangible or intangible. Those that are tangible are things like statues, cars, houses, and so forth. Those that are intangible are things like gambling, working, serving, and the like. When our service to God moves off-center (or away from the godly purpose for doing it), then it becomes a time-consuming habit and an idol. What both types have in common is they come between God and His children, severing the relationship He has with them. Our children or spouses can also become our idols. Singing in the choir or volunteering at the hospital or nursing home can become an idol as well. Anything a person loves more than God is an idol. If you feel like you're chasing your tail, then know that the busy demon is upon you. What he does is he takes the string of circumstance and wraps it around you, and then he gives it a jerk. You then become like a spinning top, going around and around in the same place. When you get that feeling, you need to realize that the busy demon is upon you.

So watch out before God turns you over to a reprobate mind. Learn to stop your world and spend time alone with God on a regular basis. What's more important than your tithes, offerings, volunteering, and good deeds is the time you spend with God and Christ.

He moved away but called her daily to check on and talk with her, but she would quickly get off the phone with him because of her husband and all the things she had to do. Finally, they had a falling-out, and the brother decided to abandon their close relationship as his pain became too great for him to handle. He tried many times to talk with her about her being too busy for even God. On the Internet, he read this story about Satan holding a convention. Here's the story.

Satan Called a Worldwide Convention

In his opening address to his evil angels, Satan said, "We can't keep the Christians from going to church. We can't keep them from reading their Bibles and knowing the truth. We can't even keep them from forming an intimate, abiding relationship experience in Christ. If they gain that connection with Jesus, our power over them is broken.

"So, let them go to their churches; let them have their conservative lifestyles, but steal their time, so they can't gain that relationship with Jesus Christ. This is what I want you to do, Angels. Distract them from gaining hold of their Savior and maintaining that vital connection throughout their day!"

"How shall we do this?" shouted his angels.

"Keep them busy in the non-essentials of life and invent innumerable schemes to occupy their minds," he answered. "Tempt them to spend, spend, spend, and borrow, borrow, borrow. Persuade the wives to go to work for long hours and the husbands to work 6–7 days each week, 10–12 hours a day, so they can afford empty lifestyles. Keep them from spending time with their children. As their family fragments, soon, their home will offer no escape from the pressures of work!

"Over-stimulate their minds so that they cannot hear that still, small voice. Entice them to play the radio or cassette player whenever they drive. To keep the TV, VCR, CDs and their PCs going constantly in their home and see to it that every store and restaurant in the world plays non-biblical music constantly. This will jam their minds and break that union with Christ. Fill the coffee tables with magazines and newspapers.

"Pound their minds with the news 24 hours a day. Invade their driving moments with billboards. Flood their mailboxes with junk mail, mail order catalogues, sweepstakes, and every kind of newsletter and promotional offering free products, services and false hopes. Keep skinny, beautiful models on the magazines so the husbands will believe that external beauty is what's important, and they'll become dissatisfied with their wives. Ha! That will fragment those families quickly!

"Even in their recreation, let them be excessive. Have them return from their recreation exhausted, disquieted and unprepared for the coming week. Don't let them go out in nature to reflect on God's wonders. Send them to amusement parks, sporting events, concerts and movies instead. Keep them busy, busy, busy! And when they meet for spiritual fellowship, involve them in gossip and small talk so that they leave with troubled consciences and unsettled emotions.

"Go ahead, let them be involved in soul winning; but crowd their lives with so many good causes they have no time to seek power from Jesus. Soon they will be working in their own strength, sacrificing their health and family for the good of the cause. It will work! It will work!"

It was quite a convention. The evil angels went eagerly to their assignments.

They made Christians more busy and more rushed. I guess the question is this: Has the devil been successful at his scheme? You be the judge! Does *busy* mean

---

B-eing U-nder S-atan's Y-oke?

This story spoke to him, causing him to have a great revelation. How many of us are too busy being busy? How many of us have lost sight of the things that are really important in life? How many of us are destroying key relationships because we're busy with being busy? How many children feel abandoned and alone because their parents are so busy? How many elderly parents only hear from their children on holidays or special occasions? When we cross over, what will God say to us about our priorities and how we spent our time? Did we value the things money could buy or the things money couldn't? Did we take the time to find a quiet place and attempt to listen to Him and what He's saying to us, or did we simply do all the talking and never gave him a chance to speak? Just because we can hear doesn't mean we know how to listen, for listening is a skill we have to learn; unfortunately, many of us will live and die while never giving that a thought. I wonder how many marriages could have been saved if spouses learned how to listen better. I wonder how many suicides could have been prevented if somebody wasn't too busy being busy and had taken the time to listen. The most important part of any relationship is effective communication—not sex or money. When we can hear not only what's said but also what's not said, then we are on our way to becoming effective listeners. The problem is that listening requires giving of ourselves, and most of us have forgotten how to do that or never knew in the first place. We spend more time on the job, at the gym, at the game, at bingo, at the mall, in front of the TV, or maybe riding a bar stool than considering the question "Am I too busy being busy for my mate, my children, my parents, my family, and even God and/or Christ?"

The Bible tells us that Christ had a problem with the church of Ephesus (Revelation 2:1–5). While Christ applauded some of the things they had done, He chastised them for the things they used to do but ceased doing. It says that they had left their first love. Their first love was having time for God and being clear on what really pleased God. How can we love one another as He loves us if we never take the time to even listen to one another? After all, doesn't Christ listen to us, and are we not to seek to be made in His image? The church at Ephesus was so busy with doing what they thought God wanted that they didn't have time to seek His face and make it a priority. Things are not more important than people. Christ is not coming back for things. He's coming back for the souls that inhabit the bodies of people. Almighty God has a prescription for the human condition of "too busy being busy," and it comes as a liquid or a pill. The liquid is called sickness and affliction; sometimes He has to put a person on their back before they will ever look up. And the pill is called a coffin; that's why they bury a person faceup rather than facedown. If you won't hear Him and what He's trying to tell you because you're too busy being busy, then you leave Him no choice but to administer the medication to you.

Life will be the mother holding you down in the lap of the world while you get the injection that could have been avoided if you had not been too busy being busy. The sister was so busy that she didn't have the time to hear his words, leaving her little brother no other choice but to write this story. Perhaps she'll read it and the Holy Spirit will give her realizations and revelations, fulfilling the hopes of her brother. And maybe, just maybe, you will do the same if you determine that you are, in fact, too busy being busy (a call that only you and God can make).

The End

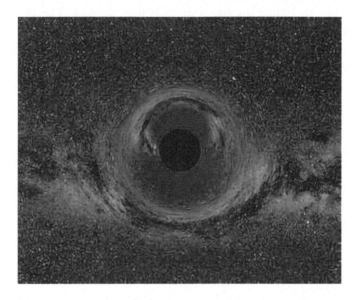

Metatron (the secretary of God) carried out the task at hand; he had to assemble the team necessary to bring into reality something that hadn't been experienced since the very beginning of Heaven and Earth. I, Reveileb, was both honored and humbled to be his intern on this secret project, which was a result of the great rebellion that took place in Heaven. While I was in my comfort zone in Paradise, Enoch sought me out because of my reverence for the Father and the Son and my curiosity of the structure and activities of Heaven. He informed me that souls deserving notification were selected for this new program in Heaven; they were to be the understudies of those in charge of different factions of the afterlife. In this program, an intern could be placed on assignment in the past, the present, or even the future to either observe or participate in events. When I was on earth and clothed in flesh, I was a blind coin collector living near Tibet. Arriving here after my death was not a surprise because I trusted in God and His Word and believed that Jesus had been raised from the dead by Him and that He ascended into Heaven. After introducing me to Archangels Orifiel and Zarachiel, two members of the team, I was escorted into the presence of Metatron himself, who asked me if I was up to the project. I quickly answered, "Yes, sir."

"Lucifer," he said "has committed blasphemous rebellion, and it's insufficient that he and his minions are simply exiled from Heaven. Has anyone given any thought to the fact that the Almighty had to create a special place of punishment for him, his operatives, and all those whom he deceived? A unique place of containment and misery in and of itself is not enough.

"There must be something more that will go along with the punishment. Something greater and more fitting needs to be created to discourage anyone or anything from ever attempting to overthrow Him and usurp His authority. This calls for a special condition to accompany the awful place of torment and punishment. One of the team members suggested to me a concept called Nothingness. I think he's headed in the right direction, but I have a problem with the idea. Nothingness speaks of nonexistence and unconsciousness. If Satan and his bunch become nonexistent and unconscious, then they will not feel or experience the pains of their punishment. Therefore, that's not desirable and won't satisfy the goal or objective.

"Let's go over what we already know. At one time, there was no Hell. There was only Heaven and we angels. Yahweh continued with His creation and created legions upon legions of angels and organized us into nine choirs—angels, archangels, principalities, dominions, powers, virtues, thrones, cherubim, and seraphim. Seraphim are the highest order or choir of angels. They are the angels who are attendants or guardians before the throne of God. They praise God continuously, calling, 'Holy, holy, holy is the Lord of Hosts.' The only Bible reference about them is Isaiah 6:1–7. One of them touched Isaiah's lips with a live coal from the altar, cleansing him of sin. Keep in mind that Yeshua Hamashiach had not been born yet. Mankind could not be cleansed of sin without a savior, but in this one instance, God saw fit to give a seraphim the power to remove Isaiah's sin with the coal. Seraphim have six wings. Two cover their faces, two cover their feet, and two are for flying. Their faces are covered, for not even they are strong enough, worthy enough, or powerful enough to behold the glory of God and His majesty continuously without being entirely consumed. Their wings shield their bodies while facilitating flight, and I have no idea what the wings are made of. No matter what the rank or the choir, there's something that none of us can do without, and that is the light that radiates from the presence of God. In it, there is everything, for there is power, there is peace, and there is prosperity.

"We know that there are seven floors or levels of Heaven, and they are occupied by and assigned to members of the various choirs. The seventh contains thrones—the thrones of the Father and of the Son being the two principal ones."

I asked Metatron to explain to me the significance of all the choirs, and He said, "I will start from the top and work down. There are three spheres, and the first sphere contains the highest order of angels or choirs, which is called the seraphim. Seraphim are the caretakers of the throne of Almighty God. They praise Him continuously. Next, you have the cherubim—not to be confused with the putti. Putti are the angels that look like babies and are traditionally thought of as cherubim. Cherubim have four conjoined wings and four faces—one of an ox, one of a man, one of a lion, and one of an eagle. The wings are covered with eyes, and they have the body of a lion with the feet of an ox. They guard the way to the Tree of Life in the garden of Eden. Then you have the erelim or ophanim, also known as the elders. They are the celestial beings mentioned in Colossians 1:16. They are the living symbols of God's justice and authority and have a throne as one of their symbols, which is why they are called thrones. The oraphim are strange-looking—even for celestial beings—for they appear as wheels in a wheel with the rims filled with eyes, and they are emerald-colored.

"The second sphere of angels is made up of heavenly lords or governors. Beginning with dominions, also known as hashmallim, they are celestial beings that regulate the duties of lower angels. Rarely do they take the shape of humans. They preside over nations and have beautiful, densely feathered wings and wield orbs of light attached to the heads of their scepters or on the pommels of their swords. The next orders of angels are called thrones or strongholds. Their function is to supervise the movements of the heavenly bodies and ensure that they remain in order. Angels of pure humility, peace, and total submission inhabit the thrones. They reside in the area of the cosmos where material form begins to take shape because of the words spoken by Almighty God and Yeshua Hamashiach. Remember, after Christ rose again on the earth, He said, 'All power is in my hands.' He said 'all power,' not 'some power.' That means that He, like the Father, can speak things into existence. Angels have some power, but there is not one angel that has all power. Only the Father and the Son have all power, and the Son has already told you that the Father is greater than He. The lower choirs of angels need the thrones in order to be able to have access to God. Powers and authorities are the last order in the second sphere. They are the bearers of conscience and the keepers of history. This is the warrior class of angels and is assigned to oversee the distribution of power among men.

"In the third sphere, the principalities or rulers are the highest order, and they collaborate with the powers and authorities. They carry out any order given to them by dominions and dispense blessings in the physical world. They oversee groups of people and are the educators and guardians on earth. They inspire human beings to reach great heights if they are allowed to. In the middle order of the third sphere are the archangels, also known as chief angels. The seven archangels that are forever before the presence of God are Gabriel, Michael, Raphael, Uriel, Raguel, Remiel, and Saraqael. These angels are guardians of countries and nations and are concerned with politics, commerce, military matters, and so forth. Finally, the lowest order of the angelic choirs are made up of angels. They are the guardian angels of human beings that you hear about so much. There are different ones with different functions. Those are the angelic choirs in a nutshell, and I hope this helps you understand that Heaven is very organized."

After taking in and absorbing all that he taught, I said, "So you are going to create some kind of new container?"

"Let me stop you right there," he said. "Only God can create, but He gives us the power to form. Let me explain the difference: There are four major processes in the creation cycle and two minor ones. They are planning, organizing, directing, and controlling. The minor ones are follow-up and follow-through. If you were to ask yourself the question "What is this planning, organizing, directing, and controlling centered around?" the answer would be resources. We use what God has already created to form the things He ordains, commissions, and approves of. He gives us the power to form, control, and manage things but not the power to create the substances necessary for their existence. We do not make matter. We manage, change, and oversee their structure or functionality and even dictate their location, but Almighty God is the maker of all there is and all there ever will be. We learn the creative processes and how to master them from the Father. Only He and Christ can speak things into existence. We bring things into being through processes that require effort, for we are cocreators, not the Creator. When He said, 'Let there be light,' the substances, the processes, and everything else necessary for it to come into existence came forth simultaneously and instantly.

That is when something is absolutely created in the truest sense of the word. Everything else comes into existence as a result of the transformation of what He has already created. We already have the container. We're creating a condition that will go along with the container. It's like we've built the room, but it has a vacuum, so now we're going to go back and put air in the room.

"We also know that a portion of Heaven had to be restructured because of sin. We had to make provisions for an afterlife when before, there was no after. Not only did Hell/Tartarus have to be created, but a place that would hold souls that awaited judgment had to be built also. So we constructed Hades and Paradise with a partition, the Abyss, between them on top of Tartarus.

"While we were standing and talking, a guardian approached us and said, "St. Metatron, I have come with disturbing news. The Father and the Son sent me to inform you that Satan and his minions have launched a new initiative that is called the Great Deception. Its aim is to gather souls unto him by deceiving and convincing men and women living in the last days that there is no God."

With that, Metatron turned to me and said, "Since discoveries are being made on earth even as we speak that confirm accounts of the Bible, such as the location of the garden of Eden and the resting place of Noah's ark, the theory of evolution that was initiated by Satan is breaking down. Men are beginning to see an intelligent directive behind the curtains of creation and questioning the validity of the theoretical concepts of evolution and the big bang theory. More intelligent and educated youths are realizing that structure and organization are never the results of chaos. So Satan and his fallen have created a new initiative to make God a liar. UFOs are not only being spotted and documented, but websites show new photos of beings and their crafts that are not from earth. They have coined the term *extraterrestrial*. First of all, for men to think that God created them and then quit creating altogether is very egotistical, unreasonable, and far-fetched. That's like saying Michael Angelo painted one masterpiece and then stopped or Henry Ford built the Model T and then gave up making cars. There are many life forms and species throughout the galaxy and universe, and some are older and more advanced than others. Satan would have you buy into the idea that the creation never occurred because there is no God and life on earth was seeded by aliens. Even if that were true, who do they say or you think created the aliens or extraterrestrials? It still comes back to God being the Creator. The answer to the question 'Which came first, the chicken or the egg?' would be the chicken, obviously, and God created the chicken so there would eventually be an egg. If the egg came first, then what kept the egg warm so it could hatch? But people fail to think things through. For instance, even if it were true that extraterrestrials seeded life on earth, someone or something had to create them. Even if one were to decide that a chicken egg came from outer space, it still does not satisfy the question 'Who or what created the chicken?' This is the Great Deception of the twenty-first century, for it seeks once again to discredit the reality of God by making one believe that He did not create life, that He doesn't exist, or that He's a liar."

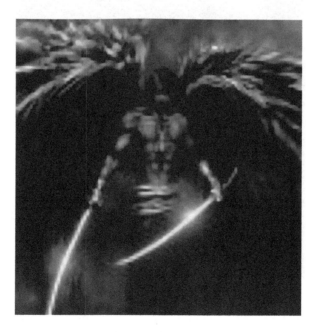

"Also, consider this—all the planets in the solar system and the universe are round. There's not even one shaped like a square or triangle. Why do you think that is? Do you think something from a big bang could ever cause such definite structure—such organization and pattern repetition? Even if it would cause just one of them to be square, it might give some validity to such a theory, but when all of them are shaped the same, it removes the possibility of chance, and the only logical conclusion is they, the planets, had to be designed to be round rather than any other shape. We haven't even explored things like gravity, the calculations that make the orbits precise, or anything else like nature and the precision of ecosystems sustaining life. The fabric of creation is but a patch sewn on the quilt of the universe and is tied into the universe. The minds of men, angels, or any other beings cannot contain all the things God has created and is still creating."

Suddenly, he shouted, "That's it!"

With his finger, he wrote out a formula in angelic script that I could not decipher, and then he called three of his subordinates to him before explaining what he needed. They vanished and then returned in the blink of an eye. The four went into a conference room, and when he came out, he came to me, saying, "Your presence and questions caused my mind to sink deeply into the center of who God is—His majesty, His glory, His omniscience, His omnipotence, and His omnipresence. We have taken four parts of forever to structure the walls of the container like that of a house. Then we took one part of the Abyss and combined it with two parts of the essence of darkness to form a realm and condition we shall call the Never. Because Satan and his followers committed the unthinkable, the unpardonable, and the inconceivable, they shall *forever* be denied the light and presence of Almighty God and will exist always in the epitome of outer darkness."

Wow, I thought to myself, *I cannot conceive of never being able to experience light. Even a blind man can sense light even if he can't see it. He can feel the warmth of it and sense the touch of it on his eyelids.*

The condition or realm Metatron and his team created surpassed anything I could ever imagine. When you think of it, it has to be almost overwhelming to consider never being able to experience the light emanating from the glory of God. Such darkness is so heavy and thick that it has to have weight associated with it. Just as the atmosphere has pressure and therefore weight, so must Never as well. *Never* implies the total absence of hope. To no extent or degree can Satan and his crowd ask God for anything He's even associated with. Can you imagine a place, an existence, or a realm so void of light that the very darkness is like a five-hundred-pound barbell on top of your head? And this condition is not temporary. When I was existing on the earthly plane, I thought I knew the concept of *never*; some people will never walk, never see, never have children, never own a home, never have a friend, never get pardoned, never get married, etc. I never knew, I never will, I never saw, I never had, I never need, I never felt, I never heard, I never laughed, I never experienced, etc. So at the end of the day, if one never meets or comes to know Christ and professes Him as their Savior and never believes in the reality of God the Father, then they are destined to get acquainted with the Never. At one time, I thought that death was the ultimate price, but I have since changed my mind. When the body dies, the spirit lives on, but what good is that if one can never sense, feel, see, or experience the light of God emanating from His glorious presence? Even a fool can't afford to roll the dice on this one. God is not an Indian giver. He gave you life, and maybe that's why He created an afterlife—so that he does not have to take it back. Although he may not take it back, he can and will decide how and where you'll spend it in the hereafter. Seek God's face while there is still time, and He can be found. Don't end up in the Never.

The End

The Recounting Scribe

I am Amazi, which means "the strength of the Lord." I was named after my ancestor, King Amaziah of Judah, who was the king of Israel from 796 BC to 676 BC, and I have something inside me that I must share with you. It beckons to come out like a woman in labor is eager to give birth. Just as the fetus can no longer be contained, so are the thoughts that are inside my brain trying to get out. I was once a Sicarius, but I threw away my daggers after I met a familiar stranger who enlightened me in ways you could never imagine. I first saw him in Jerusalem at an inn, but I met him years later outside the city of Jericho when, as fate would have it, he wandered into my campsite, thirsty and hungry.

Because of the Roman occupation in the Holy Land and long before I knew him, I had joined a secret society of assassins called the Sicarii; its members carried small daggers inside their cloaks to knife Roman soldiers, as well as their sympathizers, in large crowds. We were secret soldiers who vowed to get rid of Israel's occupier (i.e., the Roman Empire). I was a scribe, and I traveled with my Ethiopian friend, Simon the Cyrene (a Judaism proselyte), until the day he was made to carry the Christ's cross. From then on, he was never the same. The last time I saw him, he was among 120

Jews and proselytes who gathered in an upper room at an inn in Jerusalem. It was there where I first saw Tolmai.

I spent years as a scribe, researching and capturing the history of Jericho—the oldest city in the world—and preserving the memory of it for future generations. It also acted as a good cover for me. Jericho is only fifteen miles from Jerusalem and ten miles from the Jordan River. I saw John the Baptist baptize people many times there.

He was a great means for the Sicarii to carry out its objective because Roman soldiers and their sympathizers followed him both publicly and secretly, trying to find a reason to kill him. Tolmai informed me that he once lived in Jericho, and his family still owns his home there. He said that he had been Christ-curious for many years, first encountering Yeshua at a wedding in Cana where he, Tolmai, was a guest. The next time he saw Christ was when He was passing through Jericho. Yeshua had been a houseguest of Tolmai. After Christ left and was outside the city, He met a blind man alongside the road, a blind man named Bartimaeus, whose sight Yeshua (Jesus) restored. From then on, he secretly followed Him throughout the region, witnessing Him perform miracle after miracle.

While sitting by the fire and eating fish and honey-soaked honeycombs, the stranger began this oration:

I am the only man who has seen and understood the unveiling of the powers of Christ. Not even the original twelve have seen all that I have. Without understanding what each miracle signified and meant, it is impossible to comprehend and appreciate the depth of Yeshua Hamashiach's (Jesus Messiah) glory and majesty. Merely witnessing the miracles will not compel you to bow down before Him like understanding their significance will. As I sought this understanding, I became hypnotized, amazed, and awed. While attending a wedding at Cana in Galilee, I was talking with Salome (His sister) when suddenly, a crisis erupted, for the host had run out of wine for all his guests. I saw servants gather six stone water jars that were used for ceremonial washing. Each could hold up to thirty gallons.

I saw Him move toward the vessels with the disciples close behind him and then look up toward Heaven with His hands opened and outstretched. He then declared the power and reality of Yahweh the Father. An ambience of holiness began to fill the whole area, and goose bumps broke out like leprosy all over my entire body. I cannot describe the intensity of the static energy that flowed from Him to everyone and everything around Him. When the energy subsided, someone said, "Behold the power of God!" The water had been changed into wine. I was both frightened and curious, to say the least. For days I pondered what my eyes had seen, for it was as if something would not allow me to release the thought of it. One night several weeks later, while praying, I asked Yahweh to reveal to me the mystery of such a miracle, and an angelic presence I could hear but could not see spoke to me. He said that I had witnessed Yeshua's power to change or create matter and accelerate time. The molecular structure of water is not the same as that of grapes. He changed the structure from that of water to that of the juice of grapes and then advanced the fermentation process by accelerating time in order for it to become wine. I never thought of it like that. When he said that, my soul dropped to its knees, humbling me and making me hungry to hear more. I was not sure if I could take hearing the other seventeen powers, but like a moth drawn to the flame of a candle, I was compelled to hear more even if my wings would burst into flames.

There were countless times when I managed to observe the power of healing—the royal official's son, the demoniac of Capernaum, the mother-in-law of one of His disciples, and so many others. One evening, while at Capernaum, the people brought to Him everyone in the village who was sick and infirm, and He healed them *all!* Some He laid hands on, and others He did not. He healed some people without even being in their presence. Demons would cry out, "You are the Son of God!" and He would deny their ability to speak and compel them to be quiet for they knew He was the Messiah. But there is one healing that stands out from the all the others, which is the healing of the demoniac. I could see that He had the power to exorcise demons, and I saw this more than once. The first time was at Capernaum, and the second time was in the region of the Gerasenes. Yeshua went into the synagogue on the Sabbath to teach, and while there, a man possessed with a demon accosted Him. The demon approached Christ, saying, "What do you want with us, Jesus of Nazareth? Have you come to destroy us? I know who you are—the Holy One of God!" Yeshua turned to him and said, "Be quiet and come out of him." The spirit caused the man to go into convulsions and some type of seizure and then came out of the man after shrieking. I followed Him and the disciples to the region of the Gerasenes, which is across the lake. When Yeshua got out of the boat, a demoniac ran up to him from the tombs where he lived, saying, "What do you want with me, Jesus, Son of the Most High God? In God's name, don't torture me!" Yeshua then said to him, "Come out of this man, you impure spirit!" Talking to the demoniac, He asked, "What is your name?" The man screamed in a loud voice that was not of this world, "Legion, for we are many!" The sound of the demon's voice caused me and others to tremble and shake, but not Christ. They begged Christ over and over not to send them out of the area. There was a herd of two thousand swine nearby, and they asked the Messiah to permit them to enter the swine. After allowing their request, they went into the pigs, and the swine ran down a steep slope, went into the lake, and drowned.

Just when I thought I had seen it all, two things happened that proved me wrong, although they did not happen simultaneously. The first was the healing of lepers, and the second was the resurrection of the dead. I saw him heal lepers individually, and he once healed a whole group—nine lepers at one time. But when he called Lazarus from the grave, I knew that He had to be the Son of God although my position in society and political affiliations would not allow me to declare Him as such.

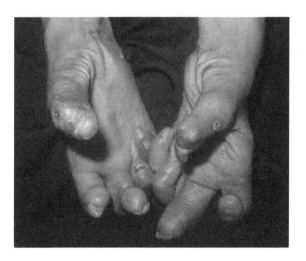

I was among the crowd that journeyed with Him to Bethany. About 1.5 miles east of Jerusalem, on the slope of the Mount of Olives, word came to him that Lazarus (His friend) was dead. Lazarus's sisters, Martha and Mary, came out to meet Him, upset because their brother had been dead for four days. Had Christ come sooner, He could have healed him. His tomb was a cave sealed with a stone. Yeshua directed them to remove the stone, and when they did, the odor of death and decay rushed into my nostrils, suffocating me and taking my breath away and causing me to regurgitate profusely. Nothing I ever smelled could compare to the stench. Many fainted from the odor, but Christ stepped forward. He looked up to Heaven and said, "Father, I thank you that you have heard me. I know that you always hear me, but I said this for the benefit of the people standing here, that they may believe that you sent me." I began to feel that energy that I felt at the wedding, and after a short pause, he commanded with authority, "Lazarus, come forth." Immediately the spirit of His friend obeyed and returned to his body, and then we heard either a moan or a groan and the shuffling of feet. Lazarus came out of the tomb, wrapped in linen from head to toe. Yeshua instructed them to remove his grave clothes and set him free. Something went all over me as I beheld the sight, for when the clothes were removed, I saw that Lazarus's skin was like new; it had a glow that literally chased the odor away. That night, I prayed the same prayer as before, seeking to understand what my eyes had seen and heart had felt. As before, the angelic voice spoke from beyond his cloak of invisibility. He said, "Blessed art thou and all that were present for what they have witnessed. It was **the power to resurrect the dead and the power to regenerate flesh**." This time, my soul and spirit were overwhelmed within me, and I fell to my knees. I then fell flat on my face as though I had been slain for the mere thought of Him and His power slew me. Like an air bubble being released from the bottom of the sea that rises till it bursts through the surface was the thought revealed to me by the angel. Finally, I understood how He was able to make the blind to see, to restore a withered hand, and to lengthen the legs of the crippled, the deformed, and the lame.

One day, I was among the multitude along the seashore. While He was in a small boat, He talked about the kingdom of God while using a parable about sowing. He often taught while in a boat or ship as the water facilitated the acoustics of His voice, allowing it to travel great distances and giving each and every listener the feeling of being right next to Him. About midday, He and the original twelve sought to cross over to the other side. I was careful to select a boat captain who could maneuver the craft to stay close to the boat carrying the Master. Suddenly, out of nowhere came a strong wind and a terrible storm. I could see those inside the boat carrying the Master begin to panic as they sought Him. They found Him asleep on a pillow at the back of the boat. They asked Him if He was uncaring of their fate and peril. He arose, stretched out His hand, and said, "Peace. Be still." The winds immediately ceased, and the waves gained a tranquil posture. I heard someone say, "What manner of man is this that even the winds obey Him?" It took not an angel to tell me and cause me to understand that Yeshua had **power over the elements.**

But that wasn't the only time the winds respected and obeyed Him. I followed Him to Bethsaida. He went there after he heard that John the Baptist had been killed. Bethsaida is a fishing village; it is where the Jordan River runs into the Sea of Gennesaret. News of His coming brought a multitude with at least five thousand men, and I do not know the number of the women and children who were there as well. He had been teaching for quite a while and healing the sick for people carried their loved ones on beds to Him, knowing He would be there. It occurred to Him that His flock had not eaten. The disciples bade Him to send them away on account of that reason, but He refused. Instead, He sent his disciples to find whatever provisions they could. They came back with five loaves of bread and two small fish; they made up a small boy's lunch. Yeshua took two baskets, broke the bread, lifted them up to Heaven, and called on the Father, giving thanks to Him. He had the people sit in groups of fifty or one hundred and gave the baskets to the original twelve disciples so they could serve the food to the people.

Every single one was fed; no one was left hungry. At the end of it all, the twelve disciples collected twelve baskets full of fragments of barley loaves and fish. As it was getting late, Christ told the disciples to get into the boat and sail off while He dispersed the crowd, sending them home. He went to the mountain to pray, and it was about the fourth watch of the night (i.e., 3:00 a.m.) when He returned to the shore. Upon his return, he saw the disciples rowing hard, trying to keep the boat afloat while they were in the middle of a great storm. I could see Him from a distance, being in my own commissioned craft, and I recognized His form. Then I saw Him walk out upon the water as if it was dry land, walk past me, and head for the disciples' boat.

He had almost gone past them when they cried out to Him, and He entered their boat, telling them not to be afraid. Once again, the winds ceased, and the waves stilled as soon as His feet entered the boat. *When is this going to end?* I asked myself, for just when I thought I had seen it all, more came. That night, as I slept, the voice of the ministering angel awakened me. He showed me that Christ had the power to change molecular weight (i.e., the atomic weight of molecules). The reason why oil floats on water even though they're both liquids is because the molecular weight of water is greater than that of oil, so the water sinks and the oil rises and rests on top of the water. So it was with Christ; He changed the molecular weight of His body to be less than that of the water and then walked on it. But that's not all. After they brought Him into the ship, the vessel and everyone in it vanished before my very eyes. When we finally got to shore, their boat was already there. I spoke with one of the twelve, and he told me that they were in the middle of the sea. Yeshua came to them while walking on the water. After He set foot on the boat, the winds ceased, and the waves stilled, and then all of a sudden, they were on the shore. This happened because He had the power of teleportation at His command. To all of that, I can only say, "What manner of man is this that can even change the density of atoms and the weight of molecules?"

On their way into Jerusalem, Yeshua and His disciples came to a fig tree, and the tree had no fruit. He cursed the tree, and after they had passed it, Peter looked back and saw that it was withered. He then told Christ what he saw. This told me that He could not only restore life with just the words from His mouth but also end it, for He possessed the power to end life. As fate would have it, a little while later, while He was in Jerusalem and teaching in the synagogue, the Pharisees and Sadducees brought a woman unto Him; she had been caught in the act of adultery. They were seeking to trap him. They asked Him whether He thought they should stone her according to the laws of Moses.

He knelt down and began to write on the ground as though they weren't there. He then stood up and said, "Let he who is among you without sin cast the first stone," and then he went back down to write. I don't know what He was writing, but I began to see the Pharisees and Sadducees drop like flies as if they were dead. Those who were with them began to leave quickly, and the ones on the ground got up. He told her to go her way and sin no more. I could see why they feared Him so because they were not only unable to control Him but also impotent when it came to the power he possessed, for he had the power to give and take life. Yet I saw another power I had not seen before. It was the **power to forgive sin.** I heard Him tell a man stricken with palsy "Be of good cheer. Thy sins be forgiven thee."

Many times they (the Pharisees and Sadducees) tried to trap him, but He read their minds and outmaneuvered them, for He had the power to read minds and thoughts. He even had the power to transfer and give others power. When He returned from the Feast of Tabernacles in Jerusalem to Perea, which is in Herod Phillip's domain, He called and ordained seventy disciples at Magadan Park before sending them out two by two into the surrounding towns and villages that He intended to visit. He then established His camp at Perea. When the seventy returned, they were joyful and astounded and witnessed to Him that even the demons submitted unto them in His name. Needless to say, I saw the disciples lay hands on the sick countless times, and they recovered as a result of the power He had given to them.

He had the power of knowing and the power to see into the future. I can't help but reflect on an encounter I had while traveling from Jerusalem to Galilee. He rested in Samaria and encountered a woman at Jacob's well. I have no idea how He knew she had been married five times and the man she was living with was not her husband. He could've only known that because He had the power of knowing. Can you imagine the shock she had when she discovered that she was flirting with the Messiah, the Son of God? And when they, Yeshua and His disciples, were in the upper room prior to His crucifixion, He told them what would unfold and how it would unfold because He had the power to see into the future.

But there's something I beheld that I still have trouble understanding, and there's but one conclusion that can explain it. After celebrating the Passover feast in Jerusalem, Yeshua and His company journeyed to the garden of Gethsemane, which is located on a slope of the Mount of Olives that is just across the Kidron Valley.

I was hiding in the shadows behind a tree when they approached. The Messiah separated Peter, James, and John, having them come with them. He then left the three, going off to pray alone twice. I saw an angel accompanying Him as He returned on the second time. Judas arrived with a multitude of Roman soldiers, priests, and Pharisees. After a brief discourse, they apprehended him, and all that were in His company forsook Him and fled. Then I saw a young man come from the shadows with nothing but a linen cloth wrapped around his naked body. He had been behind a tree across from me and hiding as well, and I could see his body but not his face. When He stepped out, I could see that it was Yeshua. How could that be? There were two of Him. The young men tried to grab Him, and He ran off while leaving the cloth behind. How could there be two of Him when he had no twin? I thought I was losing my mind, and I wrestled with that whole scene as it played out in my mind's eye over and over again. It was after His resurrection that the angel appeared to me and explained that Christ traveled back in time to once again see the events that took place. He had the power to time travel, and I'm sure He could travel into the future as easily as He had traveled into the past.

They crucified, killed, and buried Him, but He arose early on the first day of the following week. Having risen from the grave, he appeared to Mary Magdalene, whom He had cast seven demons out of. I was with the twelve in the upper room when she came to tell them, and they wept and mourned but believed not. Not long afterward, He appeared before me with two of the original twelve in another form. What I thought was a total stranger ended up being Christ, and I almost fainted when He reverted to His familiar form right before my eyes. We went back to the room and told those who assembled there what had occurred, but still they did not believe. While two of the disciples, Mary Magdalene, and I tried feverishly to convince the others that it was Yeshua who appeared before us, having the power to change forms, He appeared once again before us all. This time, He appeared in His usual familiar self so there could be no doubt. I saw the tears in the eyes of His blood brothers Jude (known as Thaddeus) and James the Lesser as they fell to their knees and worshipped Him. He chastised and admonished them because of their disbelief since He had already told them what was to come, never having lied or been wrong before. After giving them objectives and instructions on how to proceed, He suddenly vanished before all our eyes, for He either had the power to disappear or the power to become invisible—I can't say which. All I know is He disappeared before our very eyes. But to me, the greatest of all His powers is His power to save souls!

Yeshua was with us for forty days before He ascended into Heaven to take His seat at the right hand of the Father (Yahweh). Since Judas Iscariot was deceased, a replacement had to be selected to take his place and to take over his ministry as well. The qualifications for his successor were simple. The person would have to have been with them (Yeshua and the original twelve) during His ministry. They had to have been a witness to His resurrection and His ascension. There were two possible candidates among the 120 believers that were assembled. Those two were Joseph Barsabbas (known as Justus) and me, Zacchaeus, whom the disciples renamed Matthias. I have committed all I told you to writing and am entrusting you to make known to all the majesty, glory, and magnificence of Yeshua, our risen Lord, the Messiah and Savior who is the Christ and has all power in His hands. Hopefully, meditating on His power while contemplating the vastness of it all will humble believers and nonbelievers and cause them to fall on the knees of their hearts and worship Him for He is worthy!

I then recognized the stranger who had been a tax collector and knew there was hope for me. After listening to him, he led me in the sinner's prayer and baptized me in the Jordan at sunrise. When I came out of that water, I was not only a new creature but also a child of Yahweh (God the Father). It was during that time that I resigned from the Sicarii. Matthias (or Zacchaeus) left me and walked toward Aethiopia, and I later heard that he was stoned to death. After he baptized me, I was not the same, and I never will be. Can you say the same?

The End

The Eighteen Known Powers of Christ

As we read about Christ in the New Testament, we see great demonstrations of His powers. He raises the dead, heals the sick, and casts out demons. But there are many other powers that we seem to overlook. I've taken the time to analyze these subtle but profound powers, and this act has given me more insight into the depth of His majesty, the brightness of His glory, and the dimensions of His awesomeness. I have identified eighteen powers of Christ. Perhaps there are more, and I'm sure there are. Send them to me so I can add them to this section. This process of identification helps us see and understand the Son of the living God and will have a tremendous impact on one's service and worship of our Lord. It has enhanced my relationship with the Father, the Son, and the Holy Spirit. I pray that it will do the same for you. Please comment on your experience after reading this section.

1.) **Walk on Water** (Mark 6:46–51)
2.) **Change Forms and the Laws of Physics** (Mark 16:12)
3.) **Read Minds** (Matthew 9:4; Luke 6:8)
4.) **Forgive Sin(s)** (Mark 2:10; Luke 5:24; Matthew 9:6)
5.) **Heal Sickness** (Mark 2:9–12; Luke 6:19)
6.) **Teleportation** (John 6:19–21)
7.) **Create Matter** (Matthew 15:34–38; Matthew 16:9–10; John 2:1–11)
8.) **Start and End Life** (John 11:1–45; Mark 11:13, 21)
9.) **Save Souls** (John 3:16; Luke 19:10; Acts 4:11–12)
10.) **Exorcise Demons** (Mark 5:6–15)
11.) **Control the Elements** (Mark 4:39–41)
12.) **Resurrect the Dead and Regenerate Flesh** (Matthew 27:52–54; John 11:1–45)
13.) **Transfer Power to Others** (Mark 6:7; Matthew 10:1)
14.) **See the Future** (Mark 14:13–43)
15.) **Disappear or Become Invisible** (Luke 24:31)
16.) **The Power of Knowing** (John 7:14–17)
17.) **Heal Sickness through Speaking**
18.) ***Time Travel [Perhaps]***(Mark 14:51–52; Mark 15:46; John 20:7; John 2:1–11)

The Discovery

I had been playing hard that day with the sun shining down like a piercing spotlight on a Broadway stage, but little did I know that what would come would change my life forever. I was on a grassy hill in the mountains of northeastern Georgia. I sat down and crossed my legs to catch my breath with my dog, Grover. It was my habit to go to the top of Currahee Mountain to seek solitude and pray, but this day was somehow different, and soon I would discover just how and why. Grover and I would lie on the grass and gaze at the clouds as they marched across the sky, changing shapes and turning into images. Yes, some seemed to dance across the blue stage of the sky like ballerinas in an opera. Earlier, I had been at the recreation center, swimming in the segregated pool and getting a tan. There were three things that caused me to seek solitude: an encounter with the neighborhood bully, rejection from my father, brother, and so-called friends, and an uncanny urge to talk to God. I sought to become lost in the maze of the secret thoughts of my mind.

With all three occurring almost simultaneously, this was a day of days, and Grover and I sought both escape and refuge. Somewhere between the clouds changing shape from an elephant to a polar bear, I seemingly became comatose temporarily. In my visionary realm, I saw a young boy around five or six years old (a few years younger than me) somewhere in the Far East. He was by a pool and talking with a member of a caravan whose name was Gaspar. Little did I know at that time that Gaspar was one of the Three Wise Men who followed the star that signified the birth of a king—yes, the birth of Christ. I was destined to discover why he, Gasper, earned the reputation of being wise. The lad wept and cried because this day was the anniversary of the death of his only sibling—an infant brother—who was killed by King Herod's soldiers. His brother was only eighteen months old at the time. My soul saddened intensely as I witnessed each of his tears fall to the sand, and I was compelled to cry with him.

Gaspar was consoling the child, telling him of the events that had taken place a year before in a cave outside Bethlehem. He spoke of the angelic hosts that had appeared to sing songs that not only filled them with joy but also changed the smell of the air, for the odor of a stable became the aroma of roses, honeysuckle, lavender, and gardenia. He spoke of the shimmering light that shined so brightly that one could hardly see and of how everything that had a knee bowed before Him—every sheep, every cow, every scorpion, every ant, every fly, every camel, every angel, every man, every woman, and every child. Then he and his comrades, Melchior and Balthasar, approached the manger while bearing three gifts—gold, frankincense, and myrrh (gold because He was born a king, frankincense because He was born a priest, and myrrh because He was born a prophet who was destined for torture and the pains of the cross). He told the boy of how the boy's tears reminded him of Mary's tears; she cried because her baby was born to endure and then die. He said to the boy, "That was His purpose for coming here—to *die* so we might *live*." He and his two friends had now become guardians and bodyguards for the Child and his parents as King Herod sought to personally kill Him. They were on their way to Egypt, and he personally wanted to go on a different route to seek water, for they were weary and dying of thirst, but the Child insisted on coming this way. It was here they discovered the pool where both of them, Gaspar and the lad, now stood.

Gaspar apologized for his brother's death and for the deaths of so many male children; they had suffered the Massacre of the Innocents, which was perpetrated by Satan through the hands of King Herod. He told the boy that sometimes people stray so far from the light of God that they become filled with darkness and consequently used by evil. Hoping to cheer him up, Gaspar told the lad about his discoveries—the prophesy in the Scriptures, the alignment of the stars, the two companions he teamed up with along the way, the reality of angelic hosts, and finally, how he'd traveled that way before but never knew the oasis had existed. He was certain that it couldn't have been there before. But, he said, second to discovering Christ Himself was discovering his own purpose, for it had been his destiny to find the Son of God and guard him. Around that time, a two-year-old child appeared above a dune and approached them. The child parted the very molecules of air around him like that was nothing, and everything changed, for you can never come into contact with Christ and remain the same; something must and will change. As He approached the two by the pool, they fell to their knees and bowed, as did I, for although I could not see my body, I knew that I too bowed before His majesty, His glory, and His wonder and splendor. There standing before us was Emmanuel (Yeshua Hamashiach)! I suddenly and reluctantly awakened. I was filled with joy, excited, and humbled by the honor bestowed upon me by Almighty God, for it was indeed a blessing to experience such a dream. Who could imagine someone so glorious that they would be compelled to bow before Him even in a dream?

Whenever I have a strange dream, I lie still and ponder the significance and the meaning of it. Oftentimes, I pray to God to reveal to me the things hidden from the eyes of man. Suddenly, a small, still voice spoke to me, saying, "These are the things you must understand and share with the world. First, the greatest discovery a person can make is not a cure for cancer or how to rid the world of hunger but rather Jesus, who is the Christ. 'For God so loved the world that He gave His only begotten Son, that whosoever believeth on Him should not perish but have everlasting life.' Secondly, the next greatest discovery is one's own purpose, for until you discover your purpose, you will never be fulfilled—no matter where you go or what you do. We all are subject to experience happiness from time to time, but that's temporary and can change from day to day, from circumstance to circumstance, and from relationship to relationship. Fulfillment is solid, enduring, and long-lasting, giving one pleasure and contentment that cannot be found in drugs or alcohol or money or sex. Thirdly, people are born as blind sojourners in this life with a purpose, and the only way to discover your purpose is to hold on to the hem of His garment and allow Him to lead you to where the Father has planted your discoveries. Finally, there are two reasons why God gives his children anything: So that He may be glorified and so that others might be blessed."

On the way back home, Grover happily ran and played the whole way. After I ascended the three steps leading to my front porch, I walked through the front door, knowing that the rejection would still be there. The bully would still be just around the corner. I would still be invisible to the girl I had a crush on. Life would go on as usual, but somehow, I knew things would never be the same, for I was not only touched and enlightened but also fulfilled, made stronger, and forever changed. What about you?

The End

Notes:

1.) Purpose is the intent for which something is created, formed, or made.
   The purpose of a shovel is to dig, not to sew. A knife is to cut, not to knit. A river is to flow, not to be stagnant.
2.) Everything God created has a purpose, and we are no exceptions.
3.) Our purpose is not always clear and thus has to be discovered.
4.) Only God can lead us to our purpose, which is hidden in our existence, through Christ and the Holy Spirit.
5.) Discovering our purpose is the way to make a positive difference in our lives, in our homes/families, in our communities, and in our world.
6.) The greatest discovery one can make is not a cure for cancer, a new energy source, or a new way to make money; rather, it is discovering Christ and then one's purpose.

Made in the USA
Monee, IL
07 August 2023

40299347R00070